CONVERSATIONS AT RANDOM:
SURVEY RESEARCH AS INTERVIEWERS SEE IT

Jean M. Converse and Howard Schuman
University of Michigan

Illustrations by Elizabeth E. Converse

John Wiley & Sons, Inc.
New York · London · Sydney · Toronto

Library of Congress Cataloging in Publication Data:

Converse, Jean M   1927–
 Conversations at random.

 Bibliography: p.
 1. Social science research.   2. Social
surveys.   3. Interviewing.   I. Schuman, Howard,
joint author.   II. Title.

H62.C5855   001.4'33   73-15840
ISBN 0-471-16869-6
ISBN 0-471-16870-X (pbk.)

Printed in the United States of America

10 9 8 7 6 5 4 3 2 1

IN FORETHOUGHT

There are many good books on survey interviewing, written by social science researchers and survey directors, that emphasize the theory of interviewing and its ideal practice—how interviewers *should* conduct themselves in the field. Here we present the vantage point of interviewers themselves—how they perceive their problems, invent solutions, aim for the ideal, announce triumphs, and confess failures. We do not avoid offering advice where experience or research findings warrant it, but our chief concern is to present the reality of survey research as interviewers see it.

Our focus is, of course, much narrower in scope than the whole of modern survey research—a complex invention that, in effect, starts with the design of questions and of samples, and ends with the quantitative methods for aggregating and analyzing data. We focus on the "middle"—the human link between: the point at which a randomly sampled person is persuaded by an interviewer to become a respondent and engages in the dialogue that ultimately will be transmuted into data.

This book resulted from the reflections of about 150 graduate students trained in survey research through the University of Michigan's Detroit Area Study over the past decade. Students, in participating in all phases of a year-long research project or practicum, were required not only to conduct a set of 12 to 15 final interviews (after a battery of pretests) but also to consider the experience in writing. Immediately after their long week in metropolitan Detroit—with its fair share of refusals, not-at-homes, and similar disappointments—the students had to set forth their own thoughts about interviewing, in response to these vague instructions:

> . . . a paper dealing with insights gained in the course of pretest and final interviewing. This is intended to be a sensitive and perceptive account of something you have learned from the interviews treated as a social situation. Wide range of approaches possible.

That wide range has produced an enormously varied set of essays. At one end of the continuum are the poems, satires, mock interviews, and imaginary respondents of the most literary. At the other end, we have the resolute abstract theorizing of the most soberly academic. In between are vignettes, tales of terror, genuine insights, and thoughtful generalizations.

Our first intention was to collect the best of these papers and stitch them together with a little editing and contextual linking, since they seemed to provide considerable insight into the nature of interviewing that is not commonly captured by analytical or experimental reports. But the editing and linking grew. And in view of the goal of drawing directly from interviewers' experience, it seemed foolish to neglect the storehouse of questionnaires, rich with marginal comments and impressions of respondents ("thumbnail sketches" written on the last page of each questionnaire). This resource also allowed us to call upon the experiences and reflections of professional Survey Research Center interviewers, who collect part of the sample for each year's Detroit Area Study.

These accounts thus reflect *some* balance between beginning student–interviewers and experienced professionals, but there is, nevertheless, a preponderance of student voices. This poses a real limitation, but *candor* does not seem to be a problem. If, in reporting their experiences, students were constrained by academic ambition to be self-congratulatory, or overly polite to researchers, such sweetness and light is as hard to detect in their writing as it was in their day-to-day behavior. Of all the problems that researchers encounter in directing a field project, we were almost never burdened with one that J. Mayone Stycos experienced with his interviewers in underdeveloped areas—overdeference to the researcher's authority.[1]

The *freshness* of our students' experience may also seem to be a limitation to this book, since the great majority of student accounts are generalizations from a limited field experience. But this fact perhaps has as much to recommend as it has to discount it. We think that an essential aspect of the "art" of interviewing (for artist or audience) is in meeting human individuality over and over again for the first time, so that wide experience heightens one's knowledge and appreciation of the crotchets and splendors of human personality and does not erode one's sense of discovery. A thoughtful beginner sometimes can express that essential freshness better than the seasoned practitioner. We incorporate some of the evolution by which, in self-report at least, interviewers give evidence of a maturing competence. But this material is a matter of subjective impression and interpretation, without evidence from systematic experiment.

We make no apology for the subjective nature of this material—it is the *raison d'être* of the book—but we emphasize that it is not intended to stand in opposition to more objective research on the interviewing process. We cite such research frequently where it is relevant, include it in the annotated bibliography at the end of the volume, and have contributed to it ourselves. But until such systematic research has advanced further than it has at present, we see the need for a richer, qualitative understanding of this most social link in survey research. As long as surveys require interviewers to win and hold the cooperation of respondents, and to explain and manage the process of inquiry, we suspect that most of the problems and solutions discussed here will remain important.

We think this book will be of use to various kinds of readers. How interviewers solve (and fail to solve) practical field situations and how they view researchers and respondents are matters of importance to professional survey researchers and the quality of the data they analyze. For students, social scientists, or citizens in general who encounter survey research only after the color and variety has been (quite properly) ironed out of it, these accounts should provide some of the character of "street data." We hope that the material also will interest the occasional individual of catholic tastes who enjoys designing and asking questions, listening to and interpreting answers, in the survey context or elsewhere— the person who practices what might be called "interviewing as a way of life."

We express special thanks not only to the students whose work is cited in the text—Karen Schwab, Julianne Oktay, Elaine Selo, Carla Shagass, and Dawn Day Wachtel—but to the student and professional interviewers whose lively experience and fruitful ideas we quote at greatest length: Edward Pawlak, Olivia Schiefflin Nordberg, Richard Ogmundson, Regina A. Onyx, George Stevenson, Ruth Lenchek, Gary Cyphers, Helen Flanagan, Robert Thaler, Joanne Muller, Evelyn Norris, Barbara Rubinstein, Mary Sadowski, Josie Etta Dailey, John Longres, Kris Moore, Faith Fuller, Sharlene Hesse, Timm Rinehart, Carolyn Britt, Tom Viccaro, Vernon Moore, Greg Moschetti, Stephen Aigner, Diana Wright, Stanley Flory, and Mary Behnke. Many other interviewers also deserve our thanks.

Several people commented helpfully on earlier drafts of the book: Tracy Berckmans, Charles F. Cannell, Mary Elizabeth Carroll, Robert L. Kahn, and Janet Klaver. Jack Burton and Thomas O. Gay, our editors at Wiley, offered a number of very useful suggestions, as did their reviewers. Finally, we appreciate the permission from the University of Michigan's Survey Research Center to quote interviewer comments and the continuous support of the Detroit Area Study. Neither organization is responsible for our omissions or commissions.

viii IN FORETHOUGHT

We are grateful for permission from Basic Books, Inc., to quote from *Interviewing: Its Forms and Functions,* by Stephen A. Richardson, Barbara Dohrenwend, and David Klein, New York, 1965.

Ann Arbor, Michigan, 1973

Jean M. Converse
Howard Schuman

Contents

CONVERSATIONS AT RANDOM:
SURVEY RESEARCH AS INTERVIEWERS SEE IT

I
PERSONS AND PLACES OF THE CITY

A Sample of Moments

Interviewers come to know a "cross-section" of Americans in a way that many of us never do. We gather our collection of friends and acquaintances from the people we find in our own small worlds—at work, in the neighborhood, in the church group, the bowling league. Even when we get to know those strange and inexplicable people, the *friends of our friends,* we have not usually ventured very far from our accustomed ways of talking, dressing, being busy or lazy, or trying to think about things.

Granted, we run across many different kinds of individuals in the course of coping with city life. But the contact tends to be brief and "official": two people transacting some business or other, both behaving in ways appropriate to the moment of working or buying. Many Americans enliven these brief meetings with casual informality or passing chitchat. But rarely does the occasion arise for an hour of genuine talk.

Interviewers venture out of their own small worlds. They meet people they would never otherwise meet, and they often find a degree of reflectiveness, personal candor, and genuine talk that is not even an everyday occurrence among close friends. They occasionally encounter indifference or suspicion, but they leave many an interview with the experience of a fleeting but genuine friendship.

Interviewers have another advantage. For the most part, we meet even our close friends at rather careful times: when the workday begins, when the party starts, when we're expected, when we're prepared. Interviewers usually come unannounced, at least the first time. A letter describing the study has heralded the arrival, but the time is not set (and sometimes the respondent has not seen the letter anyway). If the moment is too inopportune—too private, too catastrophic, too joyful, or simply too early or too late—the interviewer will have to come back or set an appointed time. But the variety of scenes and situations to which the interviewer is admitted is richer than most of us gather up in a few days or weeks within our own small worlds. The process is one of sampling not only people but moments of lives being lived.

1

In the Middle of Things

The fact that life does not *stop* when the interviewer rings the bell is one of the pleasures (and, of course, perils) of the job. For the beginning interviewer, the experience sometimes amounts to a personal revelation. But it should hardly be surprising. In other types of interviewing, the respondent comes to the interviewer—at an appointed time, to the quiet and privacy of a doctor's or an employer's office. The rest of life is cleared away for the occasion. In surveys, the interviewer comes to the respondent who is very likely to be in the middle of *something*.

He may be deep in the shrubbery—pruning; packing for vacation; cooking for the engagement party; watching the World Series (certainly a wretched moment to interrupt). A few respondents will keep right on doing what they are doing, even if the interviewer might suddenly prefer that nice, impersonal interviewing office:

> I couldn't see him for the most part, so I couldn't tell from facial expressions how he reacted to the questions. He answered straight-forwardly, however, and had many strong opinions. I had suggested that I come back later when it might be more convenient, but he said No, *Now*. So I conducted the interview in the unheated garage, talking mostly to his legs, as he scooted around on a dolly, painting the bottom of his boat.

Some respondents will be more comfortable, relaxed, and responsive to an interview on their own territory than they would be in the isolation or antiseptic quiet of an interviewing office. One respondent agreed to be interviewed as long as it took place in his cab—he in his accustomed driver's seat, looking straight ahead; the interviewer taking his notes in the back seat. (Fortunately, the cab could be parked.) One elderly lady never did unlock her screen door; she simply talked through it after she brought her chair close to it on one side and invited the interviewer to "make yourself comfortable" on the stone steps. A part-time barber, running a neighborhood business in his basement, managed to answer questions while snipping away at haircuts. When the barber wished to give an answer more thought, he simply stopped cutting while he talked, and the customer waited. Business did slow down a bit. (In fact, it was the growing lineup of customers that occasioned the young woman interviewer's greatest discomfort; the gregarious barber kept urging her to "get to know the young men.") If such settings are anything but the typical habitat of the interviewer, they do provide a bit of environmental variety to the job, and they may even make a contribution to the actual validity of the answers. A respondent on his own home-ground may feel more *like himself,* in closer touch with his accustomed feelings and opinions, than when he is in an office, an experimental laboratory, a classroom, or such more impersonal settings that are not a part of his life and less under his control.[2]

In any case, almost any setting, including the most conventional, may suddenly break out with great liveliness:

> About half-way through the interview, men started arriving and disappearing to the basement. All very mysterious—until it started. It seems that the respondent plays in a band and they had come for their practice session. It was quite an interview: the TV was on next to us and the band music booming up from below (it wasn't bad).

The interviewer who is not accustomed to the chaos of small children may have to summon up the kind of poise or indifference with which, as a rule, only parents are blessed:

> It was a three-ring circus—the respondent had five children ranging from one to eight years and they all had a great time climbing all over the furniture. One child stood on her head on the couch next to me. I managed to hang onto my pencil, the questionnaire, my purse—but it wasn't easy!

Occasionally there is indeed more "life" than an interview can support, for example, when a woman's attention was fragmented by the dogcatcher arriving to serve her a summons for letting her dog run loose. Another respondent, very attentive and interested in the questionnaire, occasionally tuned out to check her young boys playing ball in the backyard. "With good reason," comments the interviewer. "Just as I was completing the interview, the older boy broke his leg." (Only once, in recent years, has an interviewer officiated in calling the doctor—not, as she hastily explained, because the *interview* made the elderly woman sick.) If life occasionally seems a bit too abundant, the variety of things may pose more of a challenge to the interviewer than to the respondent, as this student confesses:

> From *my* standpoint, the interview took place in total chaos. There was the radio, a record player—both on. The respondent's small son, her daughter's little girl, her husband and son (both embarking on what seemed like some rather dedicated drinking) were all there. A neighbor came in to use the phone, and there were two incoming phone calls. Except for the last few questions, she did the interview well. Chaos seemed an everyday occurrence, and my respondent knew how to deal with it.

. . . And we should have devalued the dollar three years ago!

One poised respondent apologized for her talking bird's bad manners but seemed otherwise unperturbed that every time she answered a question, the irrepressible bird was moved to squawk, "Aww, shut up." Another respondent withdrew from the living room every now and then to slap and scream at her adult nephew—"Meanest man on earth when he's drinking that beer!"—but from each such exercise of domestic discipline, she returned to the interview with utter calm, resuming the questions with great interest and cogency.

Most often, of course, the interview takes place away from the total action of family life, in the quiet of some room from which the rest of the family politely withdraws. In a recent study, for example, over half the interviews were conducted with the respondent alone. In the remainder, other family members were present but in only 6 percent did the interviewer judge there to be an effect on the respondent's answers. (Needless to say, these interviewer estimates cannot be taken entirely at face value. There is indeed a long tradition of research that illuminates social influences on the expression of attitudes—without yet much application to experiment in the *survey* context.) In any case, interviewers are urged to arrange complete privacy, but this is obviously not always possible.

If the interviewer is unlikely to arrive at the precise moment of crisis or celebration, he is very likely to hear and feel some of the emotional currents around those events—arriving, perhaps, the day after the first college graduation in the history of the family or the day before the teenage son's threatened "elopement day." Even more often the interviewer will find respondents reflective about their more enduring personal situations —a man caring for his five sons "no longer so remorseful about his divorce"; a woman reflecting on the personality differences of her girls; a father worried about his son on the way to Vietnam.

Moments of Leisure

A few respondents will be found at their ease (not necessarily waiting for the interviewer with open arms, although that happens too). The following interaction *may* be superior to the refused interview, but the case is open to argument:

> He was in terrible shape. He sat at the kitchen table drinking beer and was absolutely bleary-eyed, muttering and slurring his words, hardly able to focus his eyes. At the end of the interview he *congratulated* me! He said I was sure lucky that he'd been drinking because he never would have given me the interview when he was sober. His wife heartily agreed: "When he's sober, he hardly says a word." As I left, they both assured me again of my good fortune in finding him drunk—I still haven't decided.

This is admittedly a memorable rather than a typical moment, a time of recreation for the respondent and consternation for the interviewer. The quality of interviews is virtually always estimated at the time, and to date at least, there has never been more than a chemical trace of alcohol or drugs in any given study. Out of a typical Detroit Area Study sample of 700, a maximum of three respondents are found at their heavy-drinking leisure. In 1967, 7 percent of all interviews were found to be of low quality for all reasons: drinking, hearing loss, mental defectiveness, difficulty with English, or constant interruptions. Ninety-three percent were judged by interviewers as adequate or better.

If interviewers stock their memories with the most colorful incidents, respondents, too, often find the occasion memorable—not because the interviewer brings as much of his own life along, to be sure, but because the interview has been interesting and unusual, the interviewer pleasant to talk to. One formidable dowager, living in a huge house full of antiques, was concerned that her own reaction would not be faithfully reported:

> When I finished the last question and asked if she had anything she wanted to add, she said No—"No, but I would like to say

that you're a very attractive and intelligent young woman. I thought I wouldn't be able to go the full hour but our meeting has been so very pleasant that I forgot all about the time." I thanked her, said she was very kind. But then she said, "But you didn't write down what I said about *you!* I want you to write down all my comments—my opinion about you is just as important as any of the other opinions I gave you!"

Anyone interested in the training of interviewers would surely agree.

The Pleasure of Persons

Connoisseurs of the Particular

Effective interviewers are clearly individuals who take pleasure in the variety of lives and personalities. (Interviewers who do not respond in this way presumably find other work, even if the supervisor does not suggest it.) They become something like connoisseurs of the unique human personality. In their comments about respondents, interviewers are often quite open and unabashed about their delight. As one interviewer puts it, "I felt such rapport and personal identity with this respondent, I just wished she were a close friend of mine." Or another:

> Her home, modest enough, was one of the most pleasant atmospheres I have ever entered: she just seemed to light up the whole room. She was such an interesting person: when our conversations branched away from the questions in the schedule, I had to remind myself why I was there and get back to the questionnaire.

Interviewers are not without a similar appreciation for the tougher customer who resists the impulse to smooth out his prickly opinions:

> I had been noticing how "toned-down" and bland several people had seemed when they answered the question about Communists. Of course, they said, our democratic institutions require that everyone be allowed free speech—Communists and everyone else. It took one tired, old truck driver to stamp his foot on the linoleum floor and exclaim, "I know it's a free country and we've got to let them talk, but if I had my way, I'd shoot the sons-a-bitches!"

Inevitably some respondent comes along to try even the most experienced interviewer's soul—or sense of humor:

If I wanted to give up interviewing, this one would have convinced me that the time was right! He was something else! He said I had a lot of nerve when he first came to the door, said he worked long hours and today was his day to clean the house (which was immaculate, I might add). Then he asked me in, answered all the questions, and really *enjoyed* the interview in spite of himself. But when I was leaving, he started in all over again: said he *still* thought I was a civil-rights advocate and we weren't fooling him, he knew we were just trying to integrate the suburbs! Ah, well.

For student-interviewers, who as a rule work on only one study, there is neither the wide experience nor the job-selection processes that winnow the group down to those who find most temperamental satisfaction in the job. So the pleasure that students report from their limited field experience is striking. Recently, when students were asked specifically to rate their personal satisfaction with each interview, "some enjoyment" or "a great deal" was reported on 80 percent of the interviews. Only 5 percent were "disliked"—sometimes because the respondent was suspicious or hostile, but also because the situation was difficult and the interviewer was disappointed in his own ability to manage time pressures or lack of privacy.

Students were less enthusiastic about a recent questionnaire that focused on whites' attitudes toward blacks and racial problems. Rather more liberal on race than the population as a whole, students sometimes encountered attitudes they found appalling. (They knew of such attitudes intellectually, of course, but they had also been sheltered from personal experience with the full range of racial feeling in the United States.) [3] Some students reported that they had to exercise special control to suppress their own feelings of "prejudice-against-the-prejudiced." And for some, maintaining a personal neutrality was a stern test, as a young man reports: "To sit there with a pleasant and agreeable expression on your face—even a full smile—and listen to opinions that are highly disagreeable to you personally. Not easy!" The same student-interviewer confesses that the discipline works two ways:

> Even more difficult is the task of maintaining the objectively neutral face when the respondent says something that you wholeheartedly agree with and you want to jump up and down and cheer because your faith in humanity has just been restored!

There is, nevertheless, some evidence for believing that student-interviewers neither scowl with disapproval nor jump up and down with delight but indeed discipline their personal reactions to respondents' views as successfully as professional interviewers do. At least, systematic comparisons of the results obtained by the two groups show few differences.[4]

If the professional interviewer can bring a seasoned skill and wide experience that the student cannot offer, the beginning interviewer can bring an enthusiasm for new experience as he learns (or relearns) something about the wider world beyond the university. One intense young interviewer records his own sense of revelation this way:

> One begins to wonder—could it be that these alternative conceptualizations of reality may have some grain of truth? Could it be that those values, different from mine, may be as legitimate as mine? Sitting in the university, one can see the limitations inherent in the social locations of other people and their perceptions of social reality. But one wonders, too, if the perceptions of the objective social scientists are not bounded by their own, but similar, limitations.

Another student-interviewer is less diffident about sternly recommending to every social science researcher a "dosage of 10 to 20 interviews per year, on research in which he is most interested," in order to

> hear the airways peppered by the raised voices and shrill cries of mothers exasperated by the anarchy of children . . . to feel the great strength of a man that enables him to work 16 hours a day in two boring jobs to support his family . . . to recover from the abstractions of social science, watch the grand generalizations melt into a puddle, while individuals rise in their place.

"The People, Yes!"

For these student-interviewers, a variant on Carl Sandburg served to summarize their experience as interviewers.[5]

We learned
    to turn bitterness into laughter
    to see the humor in frustration
    essential and intimate knowledge of the guts of
        a field project—a new perspective on
        surveys and survey data
We were delighted
    by the ease of administering the schedule
    when people who were strangers at the beginning
        came through with warmth and understanding
        when the chips were down

that the weather cooperated
when a respondent felt that he had won a contest when
    he was chosen by our sample
We grew
    with the realization of our own sensitivity when
        faced with refusals
We laughed
    when respondents commiserated on the difficulty
        of being a door-to-door salesman
    when we were stranded for hours at the house of an
        ineligible respondent while waiting for our driver
We felt
    for the old people who were so anxious to talk to us
    for the young ones whose marriages were crumbling
        before our eyes
We cried
    for children beaten by their parents and for the
        bruised woman too frightened to awaken her husband
    for the smell of poverty in decayed areas
We listened
    as people in comfortable homes bemoaned their
        changing neighborhood
    to factories and automation
    to the man who spent forty-eight hours a week screwing the
        bolt on the right front wheel of an automobile
            four times
We hoped
    to have better luck as we followed the Avon Lady
        making her rounds
    as we made our sixth call back
    as we fought for new cover sheets
We learned
    that people felt they could trust a small-town Iowa girl
    what a millwright and a rigger were
    to ask, *"What kind of engineer?"*
We loved
    our fellow-interviewers
    The People, Yes!

II

THE ROLE OF THE INTERVIEWER

Learning the Role

The Ultimate Strategy

In a recent training session, a professional interviewer-and-supervisor of long experience and much personal warmth appeared as a guest lecturer. Students grilled her for what she would do *if:* What if the respondent refused to answer a whole batch of questions? What if another member of the family marched in and ordered her to leave? What if a party were going on? Liquor? Dope? They kept peppering her with questions, straining to conjure up still more unholy situations. The interviewer waited for a moment of quiet, and then smiled:

> I am calling at another person's home. If I am not *already* a guest, I hope to *become* one. So I hope I behave as I try to on other such occasions—with graciousness, tact, friendliness, courtesy.
>
> As to the particular circumstances you mention, some of them have happened. I did once come upon a group of young men, above five of them, all sprawled out on mattresses, looking as if they had been doped up for days. I did not ask for an interview. I asked them if they could direct me to some street or other, and I left, to return on a less interesting occasion.
>
> I *have* been asked summarily to leave—I left.
>
> I cannot really say what I would do exactly under the circumstances you mention because it would depend on the particular people at the particular moment. All that I can say is that when they happen, I will try to behave as I always try—with respect, with courtesy.

The barrage of questions subsided.

The professional interviewer counseling conventional tact and courtesy has already achieved a competence bred of experience, confidence, and poise. She has blended her own personal attributes and beliefs in a style of relating to respondents that poses no strain to her own sense of her total personality. The role of interviewer has become a real part of her, *one* of her ways of behaving "naturally." If her advice is excellent for almost any interaction, it nevertheless reveals little of how she *got* that way.

Shaking Off Self-consciousness

Most beginning interviewers feel a strain between the way they behave "naturally," and the way they are to behave in interviews. They observe themselves (often too minutely, of course) and feel false, awkward, and perhaps even manipulative because they cannot quite make the structured role of interviewer fit with the other styles of their own behavior. In fact, the beginner can be so intensely aware of himself and his own experience that he observes nothing so well as his own discomfort. The following interviewer is perhaps a bit more insightful than many; at least she looks up to notice that she is generating nervousness in *other* people:

> In my early interviews, I began to notice that I was sending my reactions of nervousness almost by direct wire. When I felt my own manner becoming tense or unnatural, I noticed that some of my respondents actually began to behave in something of the same way—began to tap their foot, or move around the room.

Her recovery from self-absorption apparently proceeds apace, because she reports that successive respondents grew more relaxed and less twitchy.

Fearful that respondents will not accept them, some beginners fall prey to elaborate efforts to charm and please:

> I found the temptation to handle situations in such a way that respondents would like me was overwhelming. In most cases it had nothing to do with the gluey term *rapport*. I just wanted people to like *me*—for my own ego. So I nodded like mad, murmured encouraging sounds, looked terribly interested, laughed at all jokes, patted all dogs, said hello to all children etc., because those seemed to be good ways to get people to like me.

(If anything, the behavior of this interviewer has doubtless become a good deal more "gluey" than some plain old *rapport* might have been.) [6]

Whether interviewers shrink "inward" in their discomfort or sally forth to charm all comers, the separation between one's usual self and the required interviewer personality is typical of the beginner's sense of strain.

One interviewer finds that the only solution is becoming reacquainted with a sensible soul:

> When I got back into the car and headed for the hotel, I found myself driving with exaggerated gestures, singing along with the radio at the top of my lungs, talking loudly to myself and laughing about this first day with great relief. It was almost as if I were reveling in this opportunity to be with my usual self again. For so many hours I had had to read a structured questionnaire and record responses which radically differed from my own attitudes, remaining neutral the while. I had had to present myself as a Proper, Clean-cut Young Lady, who went about the world being completely impartial. In short, it was a relief to talk to myself again—full of strong opinions, raucous laughter, and really quite sane!

If this account sounds as if interviewing requires something on the order of a mild mental breakdown, let us allow the interviewer her particular mode of relief in mad laughter and remember that interviewers usually learn this professional role without the graduated steps that other professionals enjoy. Doctors, after all, go through elaborate rituals in learning how to behave and be treated like doctors. They have other role-models to imitate; they get new job titles reflecting their progress; even their special white coats in the hospital grow longer and longer, notifying patients and colleagues that they are deemed worthy of more responsibility and more deference. Interviewers, on the other hand, receive some training and some practice-interviewing, are handed their pencils and papers, and are dispatched to professional practice—alone, still wearing their own clothes. Only by shaping their own personality into the professional role on the spot do they learn how to behave and be treated *like interviewers.*[7]

Self-restraints of the Trade

Suppressing Opinions. The fact that interviewers are not to express their own opinions is a cardinal tenet of interviewer training, and most interviewers are very conscientious about observing this rule. Only now and then does the pressure on the interviewer get too high. In the following account, an interviewer learns the hard way that neutrality is indeed the best policy:

> When the respondent said, "Women shouldn't go past the first grade; then they couldn't take jobs away from men," I failed utterly to subdue my feminist spirit. I said, "What if she never marries or what if her husband dies or deserts her and she has children?"

I can't resist telling you—my grandmother was a Kowalski, too. . . .

I lapsed instantly into silence. I had biased the interview, in that I had revealed myself even more thoroughly to be the kind of female the respondent most objected to: not only was I working —I was *in favor of* women working!

But interviewers take note. This young woman's guilt was not enough: the gods of science further punished this wayward feminist—on the spot:

> The respondent and his wife had apparently been arguing all morning about whether or not she would be permitted to go back to work. I tried to stay out of the discussion, which continued throughout the interview. (I had suggested to the wife that the husband should really be interviewed alone, but she would not leave.) Then the wife used me as a weapon against her husband. She said that she and I had discussed the problems of men and women working when I had first come to make the appointment and that I was on her side. This was an outright lie—at least I *think* it was! [8]

Restraining Prejudice. There is good evidence that blurting out opinions, however, is a less-serious problem than unconscious interviewer stereotyping of the respondent: anticipating his opinions, exaggerating a consistency in his views, or making assumptions on the basis of the respondent's group membership and social location.[9] This may lead the respondent to answer—unconsciously or not—the way the interviewer seems to expect; or it may lead the interviewer to make errors on the questionnaire, inadvertently checking the answer he anticipated hearing. This subtle form of interviewer influence doubtless deserves much more attention in training sessions than the direct impact of interviewer opinions. But it is a more difficult and complex matter: harder to "teach out" of interviewers, more difficult for interviewers to detect on their own.

In the following account, a self-critical interviewer analyzes her failure as one of professional neutrality, without fully understanding how she has anticipated her respondents' reaction on the basis of stereotyped expectations.

The study of black attitudes on which this interviewer worked was launched in the field a year after the Detroit riot of 1967, and a mere three weeks after the assassination of Dr. Martin Luther King. It was not an easy time for a white, liberal student to bottle up her own feelings; in fact, she becomes aware of how the interviewing situation actually focused and intensified her own guilt about racial conflict:

> I had chosen to interview blacks, instead of whites, for very personal reasons that had not the remotest connection with furthering the cause of the social sciences, but I did not really understand my own motivation until I had done about half of my interviews. The assassination of Martin Luther King had shaken me to my bones. In some obscure way I shared the responsibility for it—I, the Do-Nothing Liberal, hiding in the graduate school library, laughing at the very idea of bigots and race prejudice.

> After Dr. King was shot, I thought the only hope for racial peace in this country, apart from structural changes I felt powerless to effect, lay in whites and blacks getting together to talk. I didn't think it mattered much what they talked about, as long as they just started talking. My conviction of this was very irrational and very strong. Some primeval feeling.

Her attempt to put interviewing in the service of racial harmony does not work. The questionnaire is not a good instrument for the kind of "talking" that might have satisfied her soul; and her zeal for interviewing, high at the outset, collapses. Finding that she is not personally drawn to all of her respondents simply because they are black (any more than she would have been had all of them been white), she comes to reject the interviewing context and, in some vague way, the respondent as well:

> I became bored with the questionnaire, careless of the directions, physically incapable of taking down any more of the long meaty responses, and increasingly impatient with the thoughtful equivocator whose answer could not be coded.

The pressure on this interviewer is unusual, powered by her intense feelings about this historical crisis. But her situation simply dramatizes a more general interviewing problem in stereotyping—of which, for all her sensitivity, she remains apparently unaware:

> Whenever I came to the questions about Martin Luther King's greatest contribution, I was totally incapable of going on after the person answered without stopping for a moment and saying something about how badly I felt about the assassination. When I finally remembered that I should not be doing this, I did begin to steel myself and go on directly to the next question, but I felt like an ogre every time.

One cannot fault the interpretation—the interviewer is obviously too free with her personal feelings—but it is, nevertheless, incomplete. She apparently did not consider the possibility that some black Detroiters were *not* personally griefstricken about King's death. She did not examine her expectation that all blacks would automatically identify personally and politically with his life and his death. She projects her own grief (which many but not all blacks shared at the time) with a special admixture of her own guilt (which blacks had little reason to feel). However well-intentioned and benign her expectations, they nevertheless constitute an instance of racial stereotyping. Like the "wayward feminist," this "racial identifier" was punished by personal suffering in the interviewing situation.

As to the damage done to the data by this form of "bias," we report something of a scientific pity. There is no very good circumstantial evidence with which to convict her performance. The answers on Martin Luther King that she logged are much like the pattern for the whole sample; had she toted up a significantly higher proportion of answers stressing white sympathy and racial harmony, we would have at least presumptive evidence of interviewer bias. We will never know how her particular performance influenced respondents; all we know for certain are her own revelations—that the experience of interviewing shattered her own composure and her faith in survey research to boot! She concludes that it is impossible for interviewers to obtain useful data because their own personal context is so variable and vulnerable. (We choose to conclude that survey research would indeed deserve to founder if interviewers were typically as over-involved and then underinvolved as in this boom-bust cycle.)

Confessions of sympathy are surely more appealing than reports of undiluted rage, but interviewers occasionally admit that their professional detachment is overwhelmed in indignation at their respondents' prejudices. In the recent study of white attitudes on race, 2 (out of 27) student-interviewers found their hearts irreparably hardened:

> I found my whole interviewing experience simply radicalizing! One sits in the spotless and sterile white suburban homes, set in a sea of endless green lawn and curving streets, and dutifully records the prejudices of these secure people—varying only in the degrees of sophistication and kinds of rationalization. One listens to them deny the black all that he so rightly aspires to, and one becomes convinced that the black militant has reason enough to be much more impatient and radical than he is now. Bigots are *not* such nice people!

It would be a special pain for this interviewer to find her racial convictions set forth here as a possible case of bias by stereotyping, and we can claim no more than a possible case, to be sure. There is no indication that this interviewer unleashed even in small ways the expression of angry disapproval she felt, and the projection of race prejudice turns up relentlessly in her set of interviews. But she may well have exaggerated the consistency and the virulence of the prejudice she so hated to hear, as she imagined every "spotless white home" sterile but also thoroughly contaminated with race hate. Her fervent expression may be nothing more than blowing off steam, and of no injury to the interviews; but like the interviewer just cited, this one too loses all intellectual confidence in the legitimacy of survey research and loses all personal taste for exposing herself to any further "radicalizing."

Expecting the Unexpected. As David Riesman observes, the basic task of the interviewer is to "adapt the standardized questionnaire to the unstandardized respondents," [10] but the marvelous intricacies of the unstandardized respondent are discoveries that interviewers usually make on their own: experience. Can more of this experience be brought into the initial training session? Such a process should offer two advantages: interviewers should be more comfortable and capable at the outset; the information they gather should be freer of their own stereotyping through expectations.

When an interviewer reports his own surprise at a respondent's reaction, we can be warned that he is working with somebody's overgeneralizations. He may have taken the general propositions of training for genuine predictors about people. But nothing always works—not even the tried-and-true idea that most people are reassured by the anonymity and confidentiality of polling:

Early in the week I stressed the anonymity angle, but after a while I merely gave it a mention. For most of my respondents, the questions were not touchy or threatening, and the respondents had no apparent need to be anonymous. In fact, a couple of men were really quite put off by the idea. One was actually quite incensed that we had not known his name and had sent a letter to the Head of Household. Another, who was quite resistant to the interview, began to relax and enjoy the whole thing only after I had duly noted his name on the questionnaire.

If the interviewer learns the frailty of training propositions about people, he doubtless has a harder task in exploring—and discarding—his own generalizations. Is he surprised to hear that Governor Wallace, of the Southern segregationist tradition, is a poor bet for the presidency because he is "too soft on blacks." (In what way soft? The interviewer never learned.) To hear a self-styled liberal express strong admiration for the ultraconservative councilwoman? (This interviewer did find out. The man liked the way she gave-em-hell.) When the interviewer asks a question like this,

How do you feel about gambling from the moral point of view? Would you say it is always wrong, usually wrong . . . hardly ever wrong?

is he stopped by an answer like this? "Isn't life a gamble?"

In the following account an interviewer confesses that he was, indeed, startled, and he showed it:

When I asked the question about what Dr. Martin Luther King's greatest contribution was, and one respondent said, "I don't think he *made* a contribution," I was somewhat taken aback, and—I hate to admit it—I repeated the answer in a tone of mild disbelief, as if to say, "Did I hear you right the first time?" Fortunately, I recovered myself rather quickly and began to probe for the meaning behind the respondent's statement. (He thought that politics and religion should not be mixed.)

What's the moral? Interviewers must be prepared to deal with the *whole* range of possible answers to a survey question—from the bizarre to the beautiful, from the sublime to the ridiculous. And to take them all seriously. If you can identify with the clergyman-confessor, say to yourself, "Ahh, bless me, I have heard them all and I cannot be shocked." Or if you do better

with the argot of the hipster, say, "Keep cool and hang loose."
But in any case, listen—to what somebody *says,* not to what you
think they are going to say.

Beyond listening, perhaps the interviewer can be trained to listen beyond the realms of his own response-sets. Even better, perhaps he can acquire in the training period such an enlarged realm of the perfectly expect-
able that he can hardly *be* surprised.

Our own efforts to enlarge the realms of the "bizarre and the beautiful"
have been modest, and interviewers suggest that such training be given
more muscular effort, especially in two ways. First, by sensitizing interviewers at the outset to how patently limited their own expectations and
response-sets are. Second, by enlarging the collective pool of such notions
about people by dramatizing any characteristics or eccentricities that will
crack the hard line of generality.

The specific suggestions we have collected are summarized here.

1. Sensitizing the interviewer:

● Have interviewers take the questionnaire themselves, to explore their
   own personal opinions.
● Have interviewers guess the percentages on closed questions—how they
   expect the sample to break—to explore their assumptions about others'
   opinions.[11]
● Present the range of guessed percentages for discussion, to acquaint interviewers with at least the variety of ideas held among themselves.[12]
● Have interviewers imagine in writing the most "bizarre" but plausible
   answer they can to selected open questions.
● Present these fabricated answers for discussion. (What is really bizarre
   about such an answer? What sort of person might answer thus?)

2. Cracking the generality:

● Present individual answers—as wide-ranging as possible—from interview archives and pretests in order to dramatize the range of answers,
   not just the "average."
● Role play in imaginative projections of the unusual or the "unexpected"
   with which the interviewer practices coping.

The common theme of these suggestions can be expressed in the lexicon of
social science analysis: if the data are ultimately to be used for generaliza-
tion, presented indeed with reference to means, averages, and *central tendency,* then field training should focus on the human *variance* in order to
correct for the tendency that most of us have for "standardizing" the data
too soon—even before they come in.

Discipline by Discovery. The holding of strong convictions is not apparently the tragic flaw for interviewers. At least Stephen A. Richardson and his colleagues find that although field supervisors are prone to *assume* that the interviewer with strong value judgments may well "introduce bias and distortion into the research data he collects and . . . antagonize the people with whom he deals," the assumption is probably unwarranted.

> The most competent experienced field workers were found to have strong value judgments [as reflected in thematic apperception tests]. . . . In analyzing the relations between high value judgment and competence in field work, we found that, with training, students can learn to recognize and control their value judgments in writing field notes. Strong value judgment may be linked to the "reformist" orientation of many social scientists; it may generate heightened awareness and sensitivity and provide considerable motivation.[13]

Richardson speculates that blowing off steam may be essential to maintaining the kind of personal control that is required:

> High value judgment requires careful self-control if the interviewer is to fulfill his role successfully. This may require a compensatory expression of these feelings when the interviewer is away from the field situation. This . . . may explain the tendency of some field workers to indulge in derogatory remarks about the people they are studying . . . A recognition of this need may [not only improve field supervisors' judgments but also] be of help to experienced workers who feel considerable guilt after the expression of such feelings, if such expression offends their ethical beliefs.[14]

Detroit Area Study interviewers certainly engage in a process of vexation and ventilation now and then, so we are well pleased to find that this may be associated with competence. There is another, perhaps stronger theme in our interviewers' reports, however, that we suspect incorporates something of the same self-discipline: the sense of learning and discovery. Interviewers often report with considerable exhilaration that their own personal and intellectual worlds have been widened by breaking out of the academy and walking in the cross-section.

This cast of mind may be particularly characteristic of the beginning interviewer; and it may also be more available to individuals whose political convictions are not keyed to quite the intensity of some that we have cited. From one perspective, it is an attitude that is more detached and less "reformist," but no little passion is reported too (something in the tradition, perhaps, of scales being lifted from the eyes). The following interviewer articulates a very common experience:

> My stereotype of the Evil Bigot was shattered. My respondents were mostly prejudiced, but they seemed like pretty good people, doing the best they could under the circumstances. Overgeneralizing from their own limited experience, to be sure, but don't we all? Don't I?
>
> One second-generation Polish foreman said that he wouldn't mind who lived next door as long as it was just one family. When blacks moved next door to his mother, three families took the space designed for one, and he is against that. He knows that the three families crowded in, very probably, for reasons of harsh poverty, but he does not know how to solve that larger problem, and in the meantime he is against doubling and tripling in his own neighborhood.
>
> Maybe he is really against blacks for other reasons, but he doesn't think so. His prejudice is real, but so is the logic of his own experience and fears.

The interviewer applies the sense of discovery to his own development as a scientist:

> The picture of the average man and his racial attitudes that emerges for me is similar to that which Philip Converse has developed of the average voter.[15] He has much more salient things to worry about than national politics or racial policies. He feels he cannot affect things much in the national realm anyway, and the cost of information to him is high. Therefore he does nothing or acts by habit until a major crisis forces change, and even then major change takes place only in the younger generation.
>
> But that's quite like scientists themselves, after all. Kuhn notes in *The Structure of Scientific Revolutions* [16] that one of the reasons scientists hesitate to change their basic models of the world is the great cost involved. It no longer seems "irrational" to me that people persevere somewhat thoughtlessly in the ideas or behaviors of prejudice that they learned early in their lives.

Interviewers who find this kind of discovery in the field apparently enjoy a certain personal advantage. They seem to *like interviewing more* —and more often come back "high" on the realities of people than bruised by the hard edges of the respondents' minds. We entertain what must be counted merely a faith that these more reflective interviewers also produce the necessary restraint and self-discipline as a by-product. At least their focus seems correct: the respondent himself is in the foreground, seen against the backdrop of his own life and situation, rather than veiled by abstractions of the interviewer's mind or blurred by agitations of the interviewer's own psyche.

Focus on the Respondent

Whether interviewers after hours grow contemplative or churlish about their respondents, they report a critical transition in themselves on the job as they tame their beginner's discomfort and shape up their own self-restraints. Their focus shifts in a simple but critical way. From a preoccupation with the state of their own mind and comfort, they move to attending the respondent's comfort and the state of his mind. Many interviewers record this experience as that of losing some awareness of *asking questions* and gaining some sensitivity to *getting answers.*

This experience is often described as involving two changes in the interviewer. The first is the subtle redefinition of the task, for which easy familiarity with the questionnaire is a prerequisite:

> At first I had felt myself anonymous, a disembodied voice speaking on behalf of a questionnaire, trying to bring it to life, concentrating on my performance. But when I did not have to labor so intensely on the actual questions, my task actually changed.

> In the asking of the questions, more and more I focused on understanding the answers—getting them clarified when I did not understand them, getting them written down. I think I really conveyed my new state of mind to my respondents: my main interest was in getting their opinions fully represented, enhancing their freedom to respond.

Another interviewer puts it rather wryly: "Rapport, sensitive interviewing —whatever you call it—it's finding the answers even more interesting than the questions!"

With the focus on the respondent, the interviewer experiences the second kind of change: a renewed ease and freedom in her own personality.

> I began to recover my own reality. I became a *person,* interviewing people, I was really there—seeing and being seen; able to laugh when something funny happened; able to say I wasn't writing fast enough when I wasn't; I could point out to the respondent that he was anticipating a question when he was. I

could begin to pay attention to the friendly dogs and cats and curious children, the offers of food and drink, my own misplaced materials—all the things going on around me that were not in the instructions. *I* was there.

While adhering to the standardized wording of the questionnaire, the interviewer is now able to react intelligently and confidently to all the minor events of the situation that cannot be standardized. This is surely the "ultimate strategy" that the professional interviewer recommended in her counsel to beginning students; the role of the interviewer has become one of the ways of behaving "naturally."

Continuing Cross-pressures

The interviewer is charged with the responsibility of conducting *inquiry* in something of the manner of a *conversation*. The product of the encounter is supposed to be good "hard" data—the stuff of codes and numbers and computer analysis. The process is supposed to be at least somewhat "soft"—the stuff of pleasant acquaintance. Beginners may have particular difficulty, but all interviewers continue to experience cross-pressures that would seem to be the very nature of the job.

The Pull of Conversation

The Respondent's Reach for Information. To many respondents, the interviewer is something of a curiosity. He is warm and friendly but he comes not in search of friendship—just answers. He carries on dialogue in a way that almost nobody does—just asking and asking, without talking about himself. Certain respondents try to test this interviewer-creature, sometimes in a search for relationship; more often in a quest for information about him and how he ticks—either because he finds the interviewer interesting and wishes to know more about him or because his own conversational ease requires more give-and-take than the interviewer's minimal responses provide.

In certain studies, the nonparticipating neutrality of the interviewer has proved utterly impossible. Daniel Lerner, for instance, reports that many of his highly educated Frenchmen simply would not talk to an ever-absorptive neutral.[17] He had to be willing to reciprocate—give his own ideas, even at times engage in spirited debate—or his respondents turned him out. This meant that along with his neutrality, Lerner had to give up his structured interview schedule as well.

When a respondent strains for information about the interviewer, delay is the recommended procedure: the interviewer explains that he is not to express his own opinions until after the questionnaire is over, and most respondents accept this rule of the game. Now and then, however, the respondent keeps putting the pressure on; and in the following account, the interviewer deviates from the orthodox mode of delay:

> The interview was quite ordinary until we hit the religious question, and all their anti-Catholic feelings came boiling up. The respondent was sure that the Pope wanted to rule the world. His wife started in on all her lurid stories about priests—their money-grubbing; the ones who wouldn't make sick calls to poor people; those who harassed people for contributions by publishing the names of donors and amounts. She even had a story about a priest who refused "*Second* Communion"—whatever that might mean; did she mean *First* Communion, do you suppose?—to a family's sick child.
>
> Then the wife suddenly asked me what my religious preference was. I wondered for one wild moment what I should do.

(It is not untoward at this moment to try to capitalize on the suspense. Would it really serve, right now, for the interviewer to say, "I'd be glad to discuss my own beliefs at the end of the interview. It's your opinions that matter here"?)

> I opted for honesty. I told her that I was Catholic. I also said, "But please don't let that interfere with your expressing your opinions."

"It didn't stop the flow—or should I say flood," reports the interviewer. But the conversation took still another turn, as the respondent and his wife interrogated the interviewer about Catholic practices:

> What about divorce, remarriage, and burial practices, the wife wanted to know. Had I ever gone to a Rock Mass? Had I read about the man who stood up during mass, right in the middle of the priest's sermon, and called the priest down for always talking about Vietnam and politics. Did I know that the other people in the church applauded—and the priest turned absolutely *blue?* (This actually happened in a local church, and I had heard about it—though I cannot vouch for the priest's change of color!) Finally, they got it all out of their system and we proceeded with the rest of the interview. Whew!

The interviewer concludes her report with satisfaction. She judges that it all worked out well enough. She did see fit to leave unchallenged the stories about the wicked priests, but she did answer their questions about Catholicism, to which they were "amiably attentive throughout, amazingly enough," and the encounter ended on a jovial note.

This burst of revelation from the interviewer is obviously unusual, but there is a case for considering it a better application of neutrality than a delayed response might well have been. The respondent and his wife apparently considered, of a sudden, that the interviewer might indeed be Catholic herself, and thus they tried to find out. Had the interviewer deflected the question, they probably would have been *convinced* of her Catholicism—and worried, for all their bombast about Catholics-in-general that they had hurt the feelings of this particular Catholic. Her straightforward explanation very probably served to reassure them that they had committed no offense. An outright lie would have been possible, but not without its effects on the respondent, the interviewer, and the moral framework of the survey. In any case, with the interviewer's back against the wall, and in the absence of adequate planning or instruction by the survey director, we rise to the interviewer's defense to contend that her candor was an instance of the "higher neutrality." Let the situation serve as a classic exception: if she erred, no textbook rule would have served better.[18]

Whether or not an interviewer finally discloses her own religious identification, as in this rare case, the possible effect of interviewers' characteristics such as religion is an analytical problem for researchers. When such problems loom as potentially serious, they should be anticipated in the design of the study and included in the analysis. Special steps may be needed either to "randomize" interviewers or to allow certain pairings (for example, blacks interviewed only by blacks and whites only by whites). Hyman discusses a number of such experiments, and a recent one on race-of-interviewer is described by Schuman and Converse.[19]

The Respondent's Reach for Relationship. Respondents occasionally reach out to the interviewer for sheer company and warm personal contact. Lonely people may welcome the interview, not really to express their own public opinion or to determine the interviewer's, but simply to break their own isolation, as in this account:

> She was a middle-aged woman whose children were grown and she lived alone with her husband, who was not at home. She was anxious to talk, but not really about the questionnaire. She gave answers only to placate my questions—and rapidly, as if to leave more time to talk about her family life. Every other word had something to do with her own childhood and the years in which her children were younger.

She seemed melancholy, as she smoked cigarettes, sipped on a bottle of beer, and occasionally yelled at her dog in the next room. There were times I couldn't tell whether she was yelling at me or the dog, to get the silence she wanted to contemplate and talk about her intense memories.

After the interview she urged me to stay and talk, offering me beer, pop, cigarettes, the opportunity to watch television. When I declined, saying that I had to go on interviewing at other houses, she became very despondent—but she wished me well. I wished her well, too, realizing how great an affliction loneliness can be.

The Interviewer's Pull. Interviewers find that they, too, feel some strain toward relationship. One interviewer explains that she wished to be less fettered by strict question-and-answer, more free to take up the back-and-forth of converstaion, especially in two kinds of situations. First, when she found the respondent especially appealing:

> Although I tried to maintain the recommended stance with every respondent—not being so friendly as to lose my own objectivity or bias the respondent's views—it was much easier to do so with respondents with whom I had nothing in common. It was much harder with really congenial people. It seemed that the more I sensed similarity between myself and the other person, the harder it was to resist incorporating bits of social conversation.

This is an almost classic instance of the interaction that inspires distrust of rapport,[20] and perhaps this interviewer is too responsive generally. It seems likely, however, that many interviewers occasionally feel this pull toward personalism (although in the best of all possible studies, the "error" thus produced would be small and random), and that it very probably cannot be sterilized out of survey research except at the cost of other, even more important values.

The second strain toward informal conversation reported by the same interviewer is probably also difficult to avoid entirely:

> Mere chitchat of a cordial, friendly kind was sometimes just a breather. At certain times, especially after a few interviews, I would begin to feel that I was a *machine* that was wound up with questions. It seemed a pleasant break just to talk for a few minutes, to rest at the oasis before driving on.

Solving this kind of "problem" may be the task of researchers writing certain kinds of questionnaires—a matter to which we will return—or both

—And I'm going to write the president to recommend you as ambassador to Luxembourg.

problems may be largely insoluble, if Richardson's interesting heterodoxy is germane:

> How realistic is it to expect interviewers whose behavior is highly restricted by the demands of the schedule not to seek, as one of the rewards, some of the satisfactions of interpersonal relations with respondents whom they find congenial? [21]

The Push of Inquiry

While the interviewing interaction creates pressures for warm, social conversation, the interview schedule counteracts with the pressure for cool, scientific inquiry. (The obvious solution, a marvelously conversational questionnaire that fits every situation is, just as obviously, impossible.) A typical survey schedule can be counted on to feature at least some question that will stop any conversation cold.

The Comedy of Questions. Even in the questionnaires that are decked out with a fair measure of conversational style and grace, a given question can be exquisitely inappropriate to a given respondent. "What remedy is there except biting humor," asks one interviewer, "when she's screaming at a house full of children and the noise makes your ear drums snap, and you have to ask her if she's having any problems with noisy neighbors!" Even if people with noisy children may not think of *themselves* as noisy neighbors, nevertheless for another example there is even less remedy:

> You sit in a lady's living room, look through cracked, broken-out windows at blocks and blocks of gutted "has-been" homes. You walk across a sagging creaking floor, and look into narrow eyes peering at you from beneath a dresser. Not a dog, nor a cat —no, a child. Now you ask the big question in the neighborhood problem section: "Have you had any trouble because of neighbors not keeping up their property?"

An interviewer with any measure of empathy or imagination can hardly fail to find that one painful. The only real remedy is a blessed infrequency.

Other kinds of occasional "outrage" can be borne if the interviewer is able to grin as well as bear. Surely humor saved this situation, as the black respondent and his white wife were confronted by questions of racial attitude. Did he trust *most* white people, *some,* or *none* at all? They both laughed—and he judiciously answered *some.* When the interviewer asked how he would feel if a close relative married a white person, he and his wife both chimed in with hilarity: "Wouldn't mind at all, not a bit!" Very probably the only antidote to such ingenious inappropriateness is the very dose of the comic that the respondent helped the interviewer to apply.

Questions Close to the Tragic Bone. Should the interviewer ever protect the respondent from inquiry? The question is not often pursued by survey ethics: we assume that we insure the individual's anonymity; we guarantee the confidentiality of his answers; we generally do not deceive him—and this is enough. His candid answers are the very stuff of social science and should be of no harm to him.

For the great majority of respondents, that view is doubtless warranted. But what of the occasional respondent who should be protected from his own candor? The person whose very answering seems to jeopardize some of his own equanimity? The question is a fair one, for some unusual situations at least, and an interviewer brings it for thoughtful examination.[22]

How far should the interviewer pursue a series of questions which are obviously distressing to the respondent? Though it is true that most people know how to fend off the question which is sensitive and distressing, some people do *not* know how. They are so weak or so dependent or so honest that they will go right on answering the question that they don't *want* to answer, growing increasingly upset.

To take some real examples that happened during our pretest: The man whose major "social problem" had been with the police, after he had committed a very serious crime. He kept saying that the interviewer should not be asking about it. The interviewer kept asking—and he kept responding. Should the interviewer have stopped?

Or the woman interviewed in the presence of her husband. When the interview question turned to divorce, it became clear that she had almost divorced her husband at one time *and* that there was still plenty of trouble between them. The interviewer decided to skip. Was he right?

Clearly, sociology needs data to continue to develop as a social science, and perhaps to this end it is legitimate to ask questions which may be mildly distressing to the respondent? But we do need to draw the line somewhere. Where?

The problem is reminiscent of Stanley Milgram's experiment, in which subjects delivered what they thought were painful shocks to another person. Some subjects wanted to stop—and kept saying so, over and over again, without apparently being able to resist the authority of the experimenter. As Milgram observes,

Many subjects cannot find the specific verbal formula that would enable them to reject the role assigned to them by the experimenter. Perhaps our culture does not provide adequate models for disobedience.[23]

For some people, the role of the interviewer apparently conveys something of the same irresistible authority.

The interviewer who raises the problem offers no easy solution. She is not content to leave the judgment entirely to interviewers on the spot: no more than other people can they be relied upon not to confuse their *own* discomfort with the purported distress of the respondent. She fears that if the issue is faced frankly in training sessions, interviewers may overreact and skip any question that threatens any trouble at all. On the other hand, if the issue is ignored, some respondents may go beyond that "line"—into the kind of truth that is not really the domain of the survey and that is not really constructive for the respondent.

There are certainly instances in which relentlessly pursuing a question against the respondent's wishes is totally inappropriate, and yet the interviewer may ultimately ask the question without upsetting the respondent. Sometimes it is simply a matter of giving the respondent a *choice*. If he is asked rather than pressured, the content of his answer may not really be so troubling to him. Leaving the issue temporarily and coming back later can serve to allay the respondent's anxiety. If a respondent repeatedly tells an interviewer that he "doesn't want to talk about that," that it "shouldn't be asked," the interviewer is well-advised to listen to his own tone of voice. Is he sounding like a question machine? How has he responded to the reluctance that the respondent is expressing? Some respondents may indeed be too "weak or dependent or honest" to defend themselves against interviewers who are steamrolling rather than asking their questions.

The kind of question that upsets many respondents is not likely to progress beyond the pretest. But the problem is real enough for certain situations and for a few individuals. Questions turning on marriage or children, for instance, are difficult to administer when other members of the family are present.[24] One interviewer found that he could not ask a question about satisfaction in marriage when the spouse was attentively listening in, but he could hand the schedule to the respondent, briefly, and ask that the question be read silently and checked. In other circumstances, an interviewer will find it desirable to postpone a question until, for example, a child has grown bored with the interview and left the room. This variation in the administering of the question is preferable to preserving the original order at the expense of serious influence from others.

Sometimes, of course, the format of the questionnaire is designed to insure such privacy. For instance, certain questions are written for silent reading by the respondent, who then checks the appropriate code. But when no such standardization is provided, the interviewer will exercise individual judgment that is variable and fallible in the pressure of the moment. Researchers take note.

A complex situation of clear and present distress occurred recently, and the student-interviewer brought to the explosive moment what would seem to have been peerless instant judgment. The interview had been progressing without incident, until the respondent's husband came home. He was visibly upset, and forbade his wife to continue. She grew livid: she had every right to discuss her own life with anyone she cared to. It was *her* life and *her* stay in the mental hospital, and in fact she was going to tell the young man every bit of it!

Prior to this, the woman had not struck the interviewer as a particularly disturbed personality; but at this point, in their anger at each other, both man and woman seemed almost unhinged. The husband demanded that the interview stop. The wife insisted on her absolute right to continue. The interviewer, trapped in the middle, decided to fake. He went on with the interview, in something like the world's record—covertly flipping three and four pages at a time, scribbling rather than transcribing answers. The interview was lost, of course. But he got out. And the screaming did subside. The *line* was duly drawn.

The distinction between mild distress and serious trauma for an individual is a difficult one to make without reference to particular cases. Interviewer training should grapple with the issue, however, to generate some common culture among interviewers, some of whom are likely to cut off the encounter prematurely while others may go on quite mechanically in their questioning, oblivious to the tragedy.

Role Requirements in Conflict

The Contradiction

The dual role involved in conducting inquiry through conversation is commonly set forth in texts on interviewing—without quite the emphasis on conflict that our interviewers report. The Survey Research Center, for instance, puts it this way in its interviewer's manual:

> The interviewer plays two roles . . . that of a *"technician"* who applies standard techniques and uses the same instrument (the questionnaire) for each interview; and that of a *human being* who builds a permissive and warm relationship with each respondent. . . .[25]

Or take this much briefer treatment of interviewer training: "As an interviewer, you merely soak up information like a sponge, without giving any back." The instructions continue, "You should be adaptable to anyone and gracious to all. . . . Your attitude must be sympathetic and understanding." [26] Is it fair to summarize: be as adaptable and sympathetic as a sponge?

Such language smacks of conflict, and certain of our interviewers contend that the process requires a continuing compromise of styles on the job. In the following analysis, an interviewer crystallizes two kinds of behaviors that she sees as at once essential *and* antithetical, recommending that this form of absurdity be tackled head-on in interviewer training as a form of role "marginality." [27]

The interviewer is required to be *two* things to all people. First, he must be a *diplomat:* warm, sympathetic, sensitive to the respondent—just the sort of person who in ordinary social life does not go about asking embarrassing questions because, through sensitivity and tact, he knows how to avoid them. But at the same time, he must be something of a *boor:* no sympathetic understanding of the respondent will prevent him from elbowing his way right in with questions that might embarrass or discomfort the other person.

In her reflections on her own and other students' experiences, the interviewer speculates that it is perhaps more difficult to *blend* these contradictory styles than it is to select one or the other. She sees costs and benefits in pushing either choice to its extreme:

> The cool information-gatherer will tend to separate himself somewhat from his respondents. He will maintain a fair measure of social distance. By avoiding much personal interaction throughout the interview, he can avoid the embarrassment implicit in certain questions, perhaps by asking the questions quite mechanically throughout the interview.
>
> This kind of interviewer may have more trouble getting interviews in the first place, as his first impression may not be very appealing or reassuring. In the interaction itself, his blunt style seems unlikely to elicit free-flowing answers of personal significance.[28] In sum, for certain respondents at least, the interviewer's impersonality may make it easier to refuse in the first place or to withhold along the way.

The writer suspects that more interviewers lean to the *diplomat* role simply because the job is likely to attract people who take pleasure and interest in other people and enjoy the exercise of their own interpersonal sensitivity. The possible costs and benefits of this style are thus of greater import:

> The diplomat-interviewer may well have better luck avoiding refusals. He is likely to conduct a more free-flowing conversational encounter, and to elicit fuller responses to most questions. But to what lengths will he go to avoid embarrassing the respondent? The temptation may be great to skip a question or to alter its wording when it threatens rapport. In a long questionnaire, he may well have more trouble holding the respondent to

the strain of so many questions, and try to hurry things along by shortening or even omitting questions.

And, as she concludes, at this extreme of "diplomacy" the results are disastrous for research.

In actual practice, the writer sees students devising modes of *compromise* when experiencing the counterpressures of diplomacy and boorishness. The favorite seems to be the role of "helpless subordinate."

> When unpleasant or difficult questions came up, students adopted a posture of regret, as if to say, "I'm terribly sorry to ask you this but this is an assignment and I have to. It's not my fault—it's my professor's."

Some other interviewers take on the manner of "friendly obliviousness." Often more by gesture or tone of voice than by actual words, they try to give the lie to difficulty, as if to say, "Since I am a friendly person, asking this question in a friendly tone of voice, how could it possibly be embarrassing or impolite?"

Neither of these compromises is without strain. The "helpless subordinate" may serve the student better because there is some real truth to it—more truth perhaps than for the professional who is under no compulsion to earn a livelihood specifically in interviewing, after all—but the "friendly obliviousness" requires the strain of forcing an unconcerned manner.

The student-writer suggests two main ways of dealing with the problem. One is to make the wording of the questions themselves as diplomatic as possible. For instance, if the respondent's political preferences are at issue, the question should be framed in some way that makes the respondent feel that he has a choice, as in, "Would you mind telling me who you were for in the last election?" More interestingly, the writer suggests that field training of interviewers deal realistically with the contradictory requirements of the role—by helping interviewers work out effective compromises and by instituting procedures that recognize the interviewer as a "border individual" or "detached worker." Such training practices would insure that interviewers kept in close contact with each other and with the research staff through frequent workshops, seminars, and discussions—not only at the outset of training but in the continuing course of the survey.

Maintaining the Marginality

If our beginning interviewers are representative, the role of the *diplomat* is probably the preferred one in the early stages of interviewing experiences. The "human being" probably prevails over the "technician." But is there, over time, a comparable exaggeration of the technician? David Ries-man observed in his field report for *The Academic Mind* that seasoned professionals, for all their apparent competence in getting the information, seemed to leave respondents with some feelings of dissatisfaction that inex-perienced beginners did not: the feeling that they had been handled rather "too aseptically." [29] Interviewers may well get rather case-hardened by their arduous efforts under tough working conditions and come to treat their respondents with too much technical skill. Perhaps this is not a gen-eral problem; but if the rigors of the field and the "bias" of researchers do not ultimately bend interviewers into "technicians," traditional training and field practice suggests that they *deserve* to, through the tendency to re-ward and reinforce the technically correct product more than the demand-ing and dramatic human process.

Our own interviewers report that the Detroit Area Study staff some-times display utter lack of interest in the human challenges of interviewing in their single-minded concentration on clerical competence. The following interviewer is indeed angrier about the matter than most (but in her defense, she was also rated more competent):

> Your assistants—ack! There they are, sitting in their cool little office, all neat and trim, ready to attack, and the interviewer comes in dragging at the end of the day: bloody, but triumphant, unsuspecting. One day I came back to the hotel after a wild day —three spectacular interviews, two of them beautiful and one of them an utter disaster of two hours and great incoherence—and my friend The Assistant did not ask me one word. He immedi-ately armed himself with his red pencil, checked through the three questionnaires, and found that I had failed to check one "don't know" *box* (I had written in "DK") and omitted two other positively trivial and obvious things. He rated my inter-views—my two triumphs and one tragedy—as "satisfactory with a few clerical errors."
>
> I really wanted to kill him. I didn't want to send him out into the field—I knew he would be a miserable interviewer—I just wanted to chain him to the Ford assembly line for the rest of his life.

The human side of the interviewing enterprise requires that the inter-viewer maintain two human resources at substantial levels: sheer physical stamina necessary to find the selected respondent in the first place and psy-chological resilience that continues to take pleasure in meeting and inter-acting with all kinds of people, even after being buffeted by refusals. Some researchers may well leave the regeneration of that human magic to the sheer force of the interviewer's own personality when, through their own lack of immediate field experience, they lose touch with the demands and the drama.[30]

Written descriptions of the individual respondent are one mode of bringing the color and life of the encounter back to the research office. Such thumbnail sketches, written on each questionnaire, are useful in the processing of data—detecting special conditions or attitudes that will be useful in coding responses, checking apparent contradictions, or evaluating the interview as a whole.[31] But they also provide a kind of corrective emphasis on the human side of the enterprise—a way for the interviewer to communicate that experience back to supervisors and researchers.

An interviewer with this kind of delight in personality probably requires no special measures for maintaining morale—except an appreciative reader:

> The respondent is a 78-year-old widow, living alone, her left arm and whole left side completely paralyzed since her stroke nine years ago. The house is wondrously cluttered—you can hardly see the furniture for the masses of things and papers lying around. The piano in the room is covered with Mother's Day cards that friends of her children have sent. (On my first visit the piano bore hundreds of Easter cards from friends). Every afternoon two little boys in the neighborhood go to a nearby restaurant and bring her back a hot dinner. Every Saturday night a friend brings her a home-cooked meal, and once a week a niece comes to her and does all her laundry and shopping. She is well-loved, and no wonder! Here she sits day after day, on a couch in the front room, surrounded by large pillows and covered with many blankets (even on this mild day)—wearing her fire-engine red finger nails, her red-red lipstick, an auburn wig over her own white hair (wisps of which stick out beneath, because she cannot keep it perfectly straight with only one hand). Wearing her cheery, pleasant smile, without a trace of self-pity. What a delightful soul she is.

Other interviewers report that they restore their own appreciation for personality and resist the technical bias in various other ways. One is a *group* solution. Largely as an administrative convenience—economy of time and money—student-interviewers are housed together in a city hotel during the interviewing period. Through fortuitous side-effect, interviewers make of this arrangement a freewheeling workshop or seminar. Perhaps it is best termed a Free School, unaided and untrammeled by supervisors. In long sessions over coffee or beer, students carry on their own shop-talk of the field, and many of the reflections reproduced here were first crystallized in that School. We feel that they belong to that noble but regrettably sparse tradition of social science literature that Donald F. Roy calls "damfool research experiences like mine." [32]

If most professional interviewers are not usually available for this kind of freefloating seminar, returning by night after all to their homes and families, there are variants on this practice that could well be expanded. Interviewers are currently paid for their training time and periodic seminars, but perhaps the most enlightened (or at least most affluent) field operations of the future will pay interviewers to spend some time sitting over beer or coffee to express together their own kind of "marginality"— trading hilarities and agonies of the day's or week's work in human individuality. No supervisors allowed.

Even without such institutional arrangements or group practice, interviewers invent *individual* ways of mocking researchers' sober-sided emphasis on the technical. For those interviewers who can find no sympathetic ear after a long, hard day, we commend the example of the student who took to correspondence:

> Dear Home Office,
> I have been in my hotel room crying for two hours. I just had an interview with a perfectly nice but utterly misguided man who refused to answer three-quarters of the questions and told me that getting household information was an invasion of privacy. Finally he insisted that if dictators took over the United States in ten years, all the information I was asking would be used against him. What should I have said?
>
> Bewildered

The student provided the appropriate solace by instant return mail:

> Dear Bee:
> You present an interesting thought, though of course, no such thing could ever happen. Could it now?
>
> Home

As if such a truculent respondent were not enough, the interviewer complains of a very general problem—one of even detecting at the outset those individuals who might qualify for this special sample of white males:

Dear Home Office:
My parents and my liberal education have taught me to be color-blind and unresponsive to minor differences in people like age, country of origin, and sex. In this study, I must not interview any people who are foreign-born, black, female, young, or aged. It's not just that this goes against the grain—I never learned to tell the difference. Help!

True Liberal

Dear True:
As your sociological training should have taught you, a certain amount of differentiated input seems necessary for normal orientation and even mental balance in the human being. You don't seem to have learned to differentiate, you know. This is an essential part of your training, and I assure you that after two weeks of practice, you will have learned to discriminate if not to be a die-hard bigot.

Home
P. S. While you're learning, may I give you a bit of advice. They are ineligible unless proven white.

Maneuvers in the Field

On Being Refused and Accepted

The training of the interviewer focuses on the actual conduct of the situation—adhering carefully to the question as worded; being sensitive to the respondent's thought and feeling; restraining one's own opinions and biases. But the beginning interviewer's overwhelming concern is that he will not even *be* an interviewer. What if nobody lets him in?

Most interviewers have a permanent memory of that first call. Preparing a face—pleasantness, surely. Harmlessness. Civic worth. Certainly the look that radiates the disclaimer, "No, I am not selling a thing!" No interviewer we know reports preparing a face that shines with the Joy of Interviewing—not the first time. One young man found that his car served as his psychological dressing room from which, after a self-administered pep talk, he could advance to the "onstage" doorstep with more bravado (as long as he parked his car out of view of the respondent's house). Another student confesses that he was so taken aback at finding his first respondent ready and willing that he missed the message:

> When I introduced myself at the door and the woman immediately said, "Come right in," I didn't really hear her. I just went

For the next hour I will exist but not live; speak a little but say nothing; listen much but respond little; feel pain but not cry; feel rage but not explode; feel mirth but laugh only politely. . . .

on talking "persuasively," explaining the value of the study. She had to interrupt me and say it a second time: "I *said,* Come right in."

Another Interviewer or Another Try. Sometime or other, the interviewer will not be admitted. Some refusals are final and remain so despite the interviewer's best efforts to inspire interest or allay suspicion. Surely this note left on a front window was crisp enough:

> Dear Mr. Professor—Not interested in your study. Have better things
> to do. Sorry.
>
> James A. Auburn

There is always the supervisor's hope that her best interviewer will get
through, but in this case we never did hear the views of "Mr. Auburn." [33]

Just as an interviewer may be welcomed because of a fluke—one respondent rejoiced to find that the interviewer looked just like an Army
buddy who had saved his life—he may be rejected for some very particular and idiosyncratic reaction of the moment. Sometimes the "idiosyncratic" reaction is a matter of the interviewer's sex. A young woman recently crowed, in writing, "How *could* Dave have found her 'suspicious
and hostile'? She invited me in immediately and gave a wonderful interview!" A young male stranger may indeed inspire fear but a young female
may inspire jealousy, so no way is entirely without peril.

A husband or wife may refuse on behalf of the other, for reasons of suspicion or sometimes in resentful disappointment at not having been chosen
respondent. No experienced interviewer confuses this false refusal with the
real thing, but it can surely offer as stony a wall. This interviewer managed to make an end-around:

> The wife refused me when I first came. She said that her husband
> did not want to be bothered and that, in fact, she had not even
> given him the letter because she knew he wouldn't be interested.
> I left, but when I came back later, I found the respondent sitting
> on the front porch, and he was utterly delighted to be interviewed.
> We started in immediately . . .

This interviewer's plucky persistence, unfortunately, was not fully re-
warded with a classically happy interview. The drama went on:

> We had not gotten very far into the questions when the wife came
> flying out. He discontinued and asked me to come back Tuesday
> night. I did so, and we finished the interview. The wife did not
> appear again, but she really managed to make me nervous—
> banging pots and pans, yelling at the children. The respondent
> was so nice, gave his answers very careful thought, and he ob-
> viously enjoyed the interview. But ohhh, that woman!

There are two sources of public distrust for which there is probably no
easy remedy.

> Scientific survey research seems plagued by salesmen and others
> who have flagrantly misused the survey technique, such that

householders have become extremely suspicious not necessarily of a survey itself but of the word *survey*. One of my respondents told me of someone who had recently come to their door doing a "survey of children and family life for Sutter School," and of course he was the legendary encyclopedia salesman.

The most inventive charlatan of the "survey" known to us was selling cemetery plots; unfortunately we dismissed him in utter exasperation before hearing the full spiel.[34]

The second is a more pervasive distrust and caution. Some interviewers interpret it as a literal fear of crime; others see in it a more diffuse malaise—a desire to retreat into the relative "privacy and security of one's own home as one's place in the broader society becomes more and more uncertain."[35] Such feelings are expressed by persons successfully interviewed, but they are surely shared by some of the persons refusing:

> People were on the whole quite willing to talk to me, but the distrust they expressed of others! First, the locks. Detroit homes seemed like fortresses. I learned that when leaving an interview, I might as well wait for the respondent to undo all the locks, rather than try to work my way out of the maze myself. And then the dogs. Not friendly house pets but watchdogs, big and menacing.

> There is poverty, and fear. People living isolated, watchful existences, devoted to their own families, oriented to economic gain and to safety. People who were poor had every reason to care intensely about jobs with high pay and chances for advancement, and yet people who did possess some material wealth seemed guarded and fearful for their loss. People seemed to feel that they had no surplus of anything and expected others to steal what they had. Four people warned me not to go out at night.

Or as another interviewer puts the same sense of fear,

> In one building I rang a bell and distinctly heard someone come to the door. I rang again, but no response—other than the sound of someone, there, breathing, on the other side of the door. Suddenly an amazing thought struck me. Here was I, quaking in my boots, imagining that the whole neighborhood knew I was here and was out to get me, when actually the people were more afraid than I was. People were refusing to answer the door because *they* were terrified of *me*. The picture of two people, both perfectly friendly, standing wide-eyed and shaking on either side of a

door was both tragic and comic. It altered my outlook considerably. I began to arrange interviews by first talking to people
standing outside or sitting on stoops talking to one another—
people for whom those doors would open.[36]

Beyond these impressionistic accounts, it is difficult to get good information on why people refuse—for the obvious reason implicit in the
above account. But it is clear that our own refusal rate in Detroit has recently been on the rise. In 1969, 16 percent refused. In 1970, things were
not much better, with a 15 percent refusal rate.[37] These percentages are
high: it is professionally respectable to lose about 10 percent of the sample
to refusals (along with another 10 percent for all other reasons such as
never finding the respondent or anyone else at home, for example).

Although survey outfits do not tend to bruit such bad news about, it
seems unlikely that the problem is restricted to Detroit. Our interviewers'
general interpretation seems plausible indeed, and refusal rates may well
constitute a better behavioral measure of social fear in the American city
than any *question* we could conceivably ask in the vein, "Do you open
your door to strangers?" If refusal rates stay high, researchers may have to
find solace in giving these data of defeat their full analytical attention—
comparing across cities, over time, with all the standard variables of urban
analysis.[38]

Interviewers facing their individual refusals will have to make the judgment: another interviewer or another try. But if interviewers muster all
their own courtesy and calm in those refusals, resolutely assuming that the
refusal does not reflect on them personally or professionally, they can
make it more likely that a respondent will ultimately prove willing. One
student brings to refusals what may well be small solace—the remedy of
experience—but the point is well taken:

I started out with great anxiety about rejections or refusals. After
a time I learned how to defend myself—but I think it's really
quite true. A refusal is not really an adverse criticism of one's
own personality or interviewing abilities. After all, the refusing
person usually does not even see the interviewer to talk to. It is
usually the result of some private feeling or lack of understanding
on the part of the respondent.

That interviewer learned by himself how to heal his injured spirit, but
interviewers complain that training sessions could better prepare for these
long days of the soul. They are scared that they will be refused and are
quite shaken when that prophecy is fulfilled.

Refusals are a genuine training problem. The experience is not really foreshadowed by informal interviewing experience. In pretesting, for example, the interviewer is usually free to replace an unwilling person with any more congenial spirit he can find in the neighborhood, and the psychological defeat can quickly be turned to gain. In the training period, moreover, researchers may show a certain diffidence about the subject—at least, we, ourselves, have become aware of the inhibition. After all, if refusals are accepted frankly as a fact of life, this may communicate too much tolerance and understanding and reduce the interviewers' efforts. The interviewers' suggestion, nevertheless, seems useful. Refusals should be explored in candid discussion that allows interviewers to trade information about how they cope personally with the strain of being refused and what they have picked up about how to persuade the reluctant.

Getting the Interview

Often it is not really clear why a given respondent seems unwilling. The reasons may be subtle, multiple, and the critical reservations may never really surface. Is it really lack of time now? Inconvenience of the moment? Fear and suspicion? Feelings of personal inadequacy? Unfamiliarity with this survey business? Incurable disinterest in the whole thing? The interviewer's prime goal is to stay with the prospective respondent long enough to dope out what the trouble is. The lucky doorstep diagnostician, applying the insight of trial and error, usually locates the probable cause only by discovering that *something* has made for an apparent cure. The respondent finally says something on the order of, "Well, okay, come on in." What really happened to make this possible may not be clear to the interviewer or to the respondent; the interviewer did or said *something* right, and the following cures are most often reported:

1. *An appointment could be made—or a second, or a third.* Some respondents have no intention of *ever* finding the time, but other genuinely busy persons may be willing if the interviewer is clearly intent on accommodating to that busy schedule: he makes it clear that the respondent can choose the hour. Such an appointment is, of course, never a guarantee. When an interviewer arrives right on the dot to find an empty house, only the most trusting spirit will fail to suspect that the specific time was set for the nefarious purpose of nonmeeting. But even the most skeptical interviewer is well advised to suspend his disbelief, assume a genuine misunderstanding or forgetting, and set out in search again! A few respondents have even confessed—a bit rueful, no doubt, at their own deception—that they finally agreed to be interviewed because they came to be genuinely impressed at the time and trouble the interviewer took.

2. *The time-length was acceptable.* When the wavering respondent finally asks, "Well, how much time will it take?" the harrowing ethical mo-

ment has arrived. Few interviewers report telling the bald truth ("Well, the average seems to be an hour—some shorter and some a good deal longer"). And yet those who grossly minimize the expected time in some sort of mumbly deception may well get in trouble. The respondent may well feel deceived and angry; the last half of the interview may be hustled, garbled, or entirely broken off as the respondent rushes away to another appointment.

Most interview schedules are designed to last about an hour. If this is not "long," it is at least longer than interviewers like to announce at the outset. They *are* this long because the initial costs of getting an interviewer and a randomly selected respondent together are so high that the researcher wants to learn as much as possible from each encounter.[39]

Truth telling about the interview time is complex. Some of the very people who would balk at devoting *one* hour will wind up prolonging the experience into *two*. Perhaps the most honest estimate the interviewer could give would be nonsense of this order:

> By the clock, it will be about an hour, but it is likely to be a *good* hour. A *short* one. Most people get involved and interested enough that they don't watch the clock, though a few are grateful to stop and another few could go on all day. It will be about an hour but it probably won't *feel* like an hour. I mean—

—a discourse on "psychological time" that the interviewer would probably be finishing to a closed door.

Interviewers nevertheless report using a homely application of the same principle. They truthfully report the range of time that people generally take and leave the matter largely in the hands of the respondent. Something on this order:

> My shortest interviews have run about 25–30 minutes but most people talk more because they find it interesting. It will really depend on how interesting you find it and how much you want to say.

There is honesty and practicality here. Although the interviewer will work to enhance the respondent's interest and pleasure in the experience, finally the respondent is *in charge*.[40]

3. *Somebody else was interested.* A woman who had refused on the first visit came to the door on the second call with all cordiality: "Come right in! My neighbors would not say what it was all about but they said it was interesting. I was *hoping* you'd come back." The joyful greeting is hardly the word of the representative refusal, to be sure, but occasionally someone else in the family or neighborhood provides an unsolicited ally, and al-

lies can be sought out, too. Interviewers have asked sympathetic respondents to provide an introduction to a reluctant neighbor or to leave a note that the study is legitimate. Interviewers rarely know just who their allies will be and, on their patient road to the real encounter, they may have to conduct several informal "pretests."

> This was my most hard-won respondent, I think. He was a swing-shift driver who never knew from day to day what his schedule would be and therefore could never set an appointment. My initial contact was with his mother, who was quite taken aback that she could not just tell me how her son felt about things. After I had explained random sampling, I stayed a while and we got into her general opinions, her family financial problems, and her religious concerns.
>
> She was really fascinating—perhaps I felt more freedom in establishing rapport with her just because she was *not* the actual respondent. And did she ever help! On five different days I talked to her on the phone, or stopped in to see when her son would be available. On my very last interviewing day, she called my hotel to tell me that I could talk to her son on his lunch-hour break. I raced over. I never would have gotten the interview without her.

Perhaps the most dubious helper that has turned up in recent years was the aunt of a reluctant young woman. The aunt was very intrigued to hear what the survey was like and urged her niece to go ahead:

> It will be all right. These things don't take long, and it doesn't matter what you say as long as the young man checks off something or other. He just has to fill in some box or line. There's nothing to it. You remember I've done some interviewing myself.

The young interviewer had the grace not to inquire where the aunt had plied her trade, but we wish to make it perfectly clear that she could not possibly have worked with the Detroit Area Study!

4. *The interviewer stopped apologizing.* Many interviewers report that they must subdue their own guilty, defensive feelings before they can convey confidence and legitimacy to the respondent. One student realized that he was, himself, *feeling* as if he were a door-to-door salesman, intruding on the respondent. When he began to refashion himself in his own mind as something like a census taker, his outward manner changed. Without feeling that he had become brash or overly aggressive, he took on more pur-

posefulness and poise. In his explanation at the door, he took to saying, "Hello, I'm the survey taker from the University of Michigan," rather than asking the defensive question, "Would you mind . . . ?" Beginners are well advised to scrutinize their own mental image. Can they almost see a demonstration vacuum-cleaner or an Avon kit in their hand? Put it down. Pick up a mental briefcase, a clipboard, or a census form. The shift into a feeling of legitimacy usually occurs in a process that is a good deal less conscious, to be sure. In fact, there is doubtless nothing quite like successfully completing a couple of good interviews for patching together a semblance of professional poise.

5. *The respondent-turned-person.* If the product of a survey is a mere statistical Thing (often seen to "dehumanize" individuals into faceless aggregates), the process of interviewing projects a kind of democracy of the individual. The blatant equality of the cross-section survey poses certain kinds of problems precisely because it flies in the face of our social practice and runs against the grain of our individual experience.

The practice of literal equality is, after all, something of a deviant in our cultural life. In all realms of our experience, it is as clear to all of us as it was to Orwell's animals that *some are more equal than others,* and we leave the Theory of Man as the unique, valuable, nonreplaceable individual to a Rousseau or a Whitman, without letting it much trouble the practice of our daily lives. Perhaps statistical-minded researchers would not own up to being die-hard defenders of the Romantic tradition, but they do indeed insist on a theory of even-handed equality for Man in the Sample (and Woman as well). Some critics of public opinion polling find this inattention to social and institutional hierarchy a perfectly wrong-headed disregard of the way in which the world works.[41]

Interviewers charged with putting this theory into practice run into skeptics, too. Most of us have precious little experience with this "unrealistic" view. Some of us are simply *too important* to be reduced to mere respondent status. Our time is too valuable, our responsibilities too awesome, or our thoughts too elegant and grand to fit the grid of standardized questions. For the interviewer, there is rarely an effective method of bringing these hopelessly important folk down to the level of mere random equality. (At least we can report that no interviewer is on record as saying, "Listen, buddy, in *your* world you may be a millionaire, but in my world, you are just one of a random batch, see. . . .")

More people feel that they are *not important enough* to be respondents. Taciturn men will suggest their more garrulous wives; politically diffident women will offer their more knowledgeable husbands; somebody else will do—and probably much better. "Why don't you just go across the street to that brown house; those old folks would really welcome some company." Another resistant man finally put it straight to the young woman: "Listen,

I know you're studying men's jobs, but I've been cutting meat my whole life and my job just couldn't be interesting to you." (There proved to be much new information and unsuspected complexities in the meat business.)

Faced with this kind of reluctance, the interviewer's first temptation is to press the respondent with the explanation of random sampling. Sometimes that explanation is, indeed, persuasive; but random sampling itself is complex and poorly understood. When the interviewer succeeds in such a case, it can be because he has made an intellectual conversion through his particularly lucid explanation, and the respondent is ready to give his all for social science. But it is more likely to be because the interviewer has made some sort of personal, behavioral demonstration that this particular respondent is valuable and important to him. Interviewers find that some of the most routine aspects of even finding a respondent in the first place —calling back, making appointments, and accommodating the respondent's busy life—give behavioral evidence that the interviewer really means it: he is genuinely interested in this particular person. The quality of the exchange on the spot must make the same point even more vividly, especially if the person doubts his adequacy.

Perhaps the following sense of discovery best sums it up. This interviewer not only put down her Avon kit and her briefcase and her census forms—she jettisoned her statistics book too!

> I've been going around all day with the sense that it is the unreplaceable person that is the news.
>
> Talk about randomness and prior selection and anonymity and all that, sure. But did any of that ever really intrigue the mind or warm the heart of anyone except a social scientist? Nonsense. Who wants to be a random respondent? It's the nonreplaceable *person!*
>
> I have been feeling, myself, like Ms. Random Sampling. Forgive the literary allusion, but somebody once said that a poem must not Mean, but Be.

One young man unconsciously applied exactly that identity between the worth of persons and the requirements of sampling, when he encountered a woman who was unwilling because she was "an uninformed housewife." She should *represent* all the people who were not terribly interested in politics or public affairs, he explained—and the interview was on.

Cutting the Conversation to Size

Some respondents give no-nonsense interviews: they answer questions briskly and directly, with superb comprehension, in record time. A 30-year-old-schoolteacher, widowed with young children, dazzled an interviewer recently with just such a performance. During the interview, which was sandwiched in between two social engagements, the woman cooked dinner, ate the meal, supervised the children, washed the dishes, and snapped off beautifully lucid answers to all questions—in 40 minutes.

Other people use interview questions to spin off into private realms of experience and reminiscence. How to get the respondent to *stop* talking is rarely given as much attention in the literature or the training as how to prime the conversation and keep it flowing. Perhaps the emphasis on "opening up" communication is, as David Riesman suggests, a heritage from the psychoanalytic tradition, which inadvertently casts the interviewer in the role of analyst mining the psyche of the "closed" client for well-buried insights.[42] Interviewers know full well that some respondents require nothing so much as a little closing-up.

Knowing how is especially difficult for beginning interviewers. In their zeal to gain rapport, they often have to labor *not* to give sympathetic, wide-eyed listening to everything the respondent says, relevant and irrelevant alike. When the respondent lingers with his reverie or digression, experienced interviewers resort to methods ranging from soft gestures to straight talk. Some form of gentle inattention sometimes does it—putting down the pencil, looking away for a moment, even leafing through the questionnaire. If the respondent is too preoccupied with his own thought, such soft flutterings may go undetected, and the interviewer may have to escalate up to direct interruption. One interviewer reports this habitual style of intervention:

> Ahh, let me stop you here—on your boy's experiences in high school—because there is a question, later on, that is right on the matter of education. The next question is not really connected, but I have to ask them in order. . . .

There is another suggestion that interviewers offer for handling the respondent's digression. Once in a while, *let* him. *Listen.* The respondent may indeed just need a brief breather. He may be feeling some emotional strain from a particular question, or he may simply need to relax a bit, into the comfortable shapes of his own "unstandardized" thought, from the sheer concentration he has marshaled in order to answer so many questions in succession. As one interviewer describes that process,

> I learned that I had to be flexible in response to a person's concentration ability. At first, when a person started in on a story about life in the Navy during the war, or an account of the dog's prowess as a watchman, I panicked a little: I felt that the interview was going to splinter off into small talk and long stories.

Then I began to realize that this was an integral part of the process. Our questionnaire was something of a strain for some of my people and they needed a chance to retreat from it for a short time. They seemed to need a shift in focus, and I usually drifted with them for a while until they seemed ready to return to the questions.

If an interviewer refuses to drift even a little, resisting all digressions, the respondent may withdraw or honor the interviewer with more exasperation than information, as one of these respondents does. The following two accounts are from the same study of men's jobs and experiences in the Detroit labor force. Both respondents are in their mid-fifties, old enough to have had a variety of work experience, some of it in lean times. The first interviewer reports enjoyment in hearing some of this personal history:

The respondent was very cooperative. He operates an elevator now, but he enjoyed talking about the various jobs he has had and the changes that have taken place over the years. He talked about the early jobs during the Depression, when he worked long, long hours for ten and fifteen cents an hour.

Compare the reaction of a different interviewer:

The respondent was willing to be interviewed—he has a son at the University—but he became more and more disenchanted in the job-history section. He wanted to tell me all about the Depression and how hard it was to find work. . . .

("Why didn't you let him rap about the Depression then?"—an exasperated supervisor has queried in the margins of the second interview.)
As the sketch of the second respondent continues, it seems clear that this interviewer has, at best, merely suffered the personal reminiscence, and very probably cut it off. Rapport unravels:

He often responded before I had a chance to complete the question. He often didn't like the idea of having to answer in the categories I gave him. He kept giving me indications that he knew my business better than I did, although [note the interviewer's vindictive pleasure] he was not even right about what I was studying: he thought I was studying to be a social worker instead of a sociologist. All in all, it was not a fantastically pleasant experience.

Neither, presumably, was it a joy for the respondent.
It may be that this respondent did know the interviewer's business bet-

ter, being employed as a parole officer and doing a fair amount of interviewing himself. (The two types of interviewing are indeed different, and possibly jaundiced the respondent's attitude, posing special problems for the interviewer.) But the initial contact seems to have been all right. The interviewer seems to have at least bungled the timing. He has obstructed the kind of reminiscence that is probably irresistible to a respondent who is thinking at all seriously about his own job history. Furthermore, this kind of reminiscence is hardly irrelevant to the study of job experiences, although the question of how long and detailed such an account will be is a valid one for the interviewer. The second interview was shorter than the first by a substantial amount—a half hour. But the time saved was probably a loss to both people as well as to the study.

The Neutral Probe

In Pursuit of Specificity. The activity called *probing* sounds perhaps just a bit more surgical than befits the gentle art of asking questions. But the poetry of survey research is thin; the word has taken a prominent place in the lexicon of polling and quickly enters the habitual vocabulary of interviewers.

The interviewer is to probe for additional information or clarification when he hears something that he does not understand or, even better, something that a third person would not understand. The glittering generality will turn up somewhere in virtually any interview. In a matter of a few hours, one interviewer accumulated these laconic truths:

> It's the parents.
> Lack of communication.
> Job concerns.
> They're just too young.

The *question*—"What is the main reason teenagers drop out of school?"—was probably no less vague and general and, perhaps, was the main reason that the initial answers were so unsatisfactory. Even to better questions, however, many respondents will answer with their own shorthand: highly concentrated code-words that would be meaningful in an ordinary conversation, to which a friend-listener would bring knowledge of the speaker's preoccupations, response-sets, styles of thought and language, and so on. The interviewer does not bring enough information to decode what such answers mean, and he must realize that instantaneously enough to probe at once (even when he also thinks, in *his* shorthand, that "they're too young" or "it's the parents"). Interviewers usually learn early in their experience to detect most of the uselessly general answers, first by understanding clearly the research intent of the question and then applying that knowledge to the relevance and completeness of each answer after another. There is no general procedure, other than the application of the usual virtues: sensitive listening and quick wit.

It is easy enough to practice one specific test, however—having small groups of interviewers listen to each other's open-ended answers recorded on the practice interviews and pretests. That simple process will yield useful criticisms of clarity, specificity, germaneness, and completeness. It is especially helpful for detecting the long, voluble, expansive answer that may well have satisfied the interviewer on the scene but that, in all its irrelevance, may be no more informative than minced words.

In Avoidance of Ignorance. How the interviewer is to probe a "don't know" answer is generally a more slippery matter. What does such an answer really mean? Only the dullest listener would fail to distinguish between these two extremes:

> I don't know . . . I have never given it a thought. Don't have the slightest idea. Just don't know about that one. . . .

and this:

> I don't know . . . hmm. . . . Let me see, I suppose I'd say. . . .

But there are many other versions of the same words that are much more opaque to instant interpretation. To take just a few:

> I don't know (and I don't care and I don't give a damn and this is boring).
> I don't know (and I'm not saying and it's none of your business).
> I don't know (but I do know that what I might say would probably strike you as stupid).
> I don't know (and I don't want to know and the whole thing makes me uneasy to think about it and let's go on).

Only the interviewer can decide whether to probe for the "real" answer or to record the fact that she already has it.

If the interviewer presses the respondent for a substantive answer, how many times should he probe? Instructions are difficult to standardize not only because each situation has subtleties and ambiguities that the interviewer must interpret on the spot but also because researchers themselves are often not entirely clear how they feel about public *nonopinion,* and what use they will make of it, and their instructions are likely to reflect some of that uncertainty.[43] Researchers tend to favor the respondents who *do* know, often enough discarding the "don't knows" along with the "not-ascertaineds," letting the computer whir along with the cases in which the respondent said something or other, even if some uncertain portion of that group may well have invented an opinion for the occasion. Sometimes no doubt to please the nice interviewer.

Certain professionals in the survey field argue that nonopinions are the most important matter. As Leo Bogart puts it, "The question of *what* people think about public issues is really secondary to the question of whether they think about them at all." [44] It is nevertheless a rare piece of published analysis that shows much fascination for nonopinion, as A. Sicinski has in a comparative survey of three national groups. Norwegians seemed to be the most knowledgeable and more informed on the factual questions than the Poles or the French, who more often just did not know. When he gave the data more complex scrutiny, however (comparing factually wrong answers and "don't knows"), he found another interpretation more plausible. The French and the Poles were simply more willing to admit ignorance; Norwegians were more willing to guess. [45]

Unless the researcher is very clear himself about the uses to which he will ultimately put "ignorance" (or indifference), he is unlikely to give standardized probing instructions. The interviewers may proceed dutifully enough to record all the "don't know" answers (probing them a variable number of times), and if a substantive answer is finally produced, it is only this last bit of information that the researcher will carry away for analysis —and interviewers know it. In view of that analytical practice, interviewers are very likely to exert, at the very least, subtle pressure for the respondent to rummage around in his mind for something that will serve as an opinion, and the "attitudes and nonattitudes" in Philip E. Converse's phrase will enter the computer willy-nilly. [46]

Styles of Probing. Generally suggested probe wordings are usually more helpful for crystallizing the meaning of the glittering generality than for penetrating the "real" meaning of professed ignorance. In either case, the interviewer is to select a probe wording that is neutral, supportive of the respondent, and productive of more information. Interviewer training usually provides some sort of probing glossary, from which the interviewer is to choose an appropriate sentence:

> Could you tell me a little more about that?
>
> How do you mean, exactly?
>
> Why would you say you feel that way?

Interviewers report that they *try* to stick to the probe script, but their reported experience makes it clear that their way of interpreting that script varies rather considerably. Some interviewers hang as closely to the literal language as they possibly can; others confess that they adapt their own probe language to the respondent's general style.

One dutifully conservative interviewer, who adhered carefully to the script, found that she began to amuse her respondent:

> About halfway through, in a good-natured and friendly way, the respondent began to mimic my probes, with an exaggerated emphasis: "I know, *Why* do I feel that way? *Could* I be a little more specific? Yes, How do I *mean*, exactly?"

The interviewer's language can become so neutral that it will formalize and chill the spontaneity of the relationship as it sends out signals that the interviewer is in better contact with the script (be it questionnaire or probing language) than with the respondent.

At the other liberal extreme, we find interviewers who, without deviating from the literal wording of the *question,* adapt their probing language and manner to the style of the respondent. Sometimes that person's apparent style is even more crisp and businesslike than the questionnaire itself, as in this account:

> His neighbors had warned me that he was a "loner," a "tough guy," not going in for a lot of foolishness or a lot of talk. When I approached him in the yard, he said, "Actions speak louder than words; I've got no use for a lot of questions."

> Finally he agreed to answer a couple of questions out in the yard. I asked them very matter-of-factly, using a kind of "tough guy" voice myself, trying to go along with the kind of tone and pace that he was using—straightforward, business-like, "no nonsense." I did little smiling or reinforcing.

The interviewer reports success, for soon the respondent got quite involved, "striding up and down the sidewalk, delivering opinions with gusto."

Adapting to the respondent's style *may* take the interviewer into modes of support, ingratiation or "charm" that are not written into the script—but that is only one kind of respondent. The interviewer just cited found that he was "tough" with the tough guy, warm and smiley with the grandmother, freewheeling and breezy with the young man living in the commune.

This freer probing style is presented in some detail by an interviewer who had come to feel in his pretest experience that his probing manner heavily influenced rapport. In effect, he wrote his own probing script and

Why do I think that? BECAUSE! BECAUSE! BECAUSE!

tried to make selections to match the respondent. He reported great pleasure in using probes as a quick-change artist would use costume. To take three examples:

1. *For the respondent using argot, especially when the interviewer is not sure of its meaning:*

   "The people at the University don't usually get the meaning of this language, so could you explain . . ."   *or*

   "Man, I thought I was with it, but I'm not there either. What does . . . mean exactly? I see, now I'm getting it . . ."

2. *For the sensitive respondent feeling inadequate, needing reinforcement:*

   "I sense that there's a bit more behind what you said. You're really onto something here. What do you mean by . . . ?"
   or

   "I hope you don't feel that I'm pushing you on this, but we're not supposed to guess anything, because we might not get your feeling down exactly . . ."   *or*

"I'm pretty sure I know what you mean and what you're driving at here, but could you say a little more . . ." *or*

"I've done three interviews today and I've found that people use the word in different ways. Could you tell me what you mean by 'more education'?"

3. *For the respondent with whom rapport is already high:*
"I'd like to pin you down a little more on what you just said . . ." *or*

"I'm going to have to stop you here again, because I'm not really sure what you mean . . ." *or*

"I don't really follow you. You've laid it out generally but what do you mean exactly by . . . ?"

Do self-styled probe artists of this kind contaminate the data by adapting too readily to the respondent as they see him? Are such chameleon interviewers likely to take on too much of the respondent's local color, and bring back another small collection of "nonattitudes?" (One can also ask if the "conservative" interviewer who strikes her respondent as mechanical and impersonal brings back too little of that local color.) We are not prepared to answer such questions—except to add an inconclusive footnote that the candid interviewers just cited were rated by supervisors as excellent; and to speculate that such interviewers adapt quickly to their fundamental intuition that there is no single interviewer style that fits every occasion or all respondents.

Recent work by Henson, Cannell, and Lawson supports that basic intuition. The authors measured the accuracy of respondents' recall of factual material under conditions varying both the interviewer style (impersonal to personal) and question form (brief and standard versus longer and redundant). For respondents with lower education, the interpersonal interviewer style was more congenial, in that it elicited higher accuracy—very probably, as the authors reason, because it provided reassuring feedback and reduced anxiety. For respondents with higher education, the more businesslike treatment was more effective: the interpersonal interviewer using brief-form questions produced better recall. In fact, the authors suspect that these respondents may have been annoyed by the very verbal interviewer and resisted making the effort to remember complex events; in any case, their motivation to work very hard to recall past events seemed to have been diluted "since any answer . . . which seemed to fit the objective of the question was acceptable to the interviewer." They conclude that "under certain conditions a professional style interview is superior to an interpersonal style." [47] One suspects that such conditions were presented by the "loner, tough guy" or the brisk, widowed schoolteacher.

Such a study illuminates the fact that interviewer style is a complicated business—interacting with the form of the question, the nature of the informational task, the interpersonal requirements of the respondent—and probably more complicated than some of our interviewers think when they report that they take particular pride in "sizing up a person and then taking what seems the most appropriate stance that will allow him the fullest comfort and freedom in the respondent role." Interviewers of this stripe usually have the greatest interpersonal sensitivity and flexibility—perhaps like the professionals whom David Riesman admired as "genuine virtuosi who enjoy coping with taxing assignments and 'difficult' respondents." [48] The Henson et al. work suggests that the supreme "virtuosi" must also be flexible in the degree that they exercise this flair for personalism and dramatic interaction, sometimes taming it to a very businesslike minimum.

Weaving Down the Road. "Overrapport" has been identified in the literature on interviewing since the 1950s when S. M. Miller reported that he was so successful in making cordial contacts that he jeopardized his investigation: he had become such a "good buddy" of some people that it became impossible for him to ask certain questions that would have seemed to them, by then, hostile and antagonistic.[49] Miller was a participant-observer at the time, not a survey interviewer, but *overrapport* (and lately even *rapport*) is under considerable scrutiny. There is research evidence that interviewer effect, or bias, operates when interviewers are "too close" to their respondent in basic social characteristics such as age, race, and class or "too personal" in their interviewing style.[50]

Richardson suggests two possible reasons for this current research concern. It may simply be a reaction against earlier thinking, in which rapport figured so prominently. Even more interesting to us is Richardson's second speculation that it may be

> an idealization stemming directly from the demands of standardization in the schedule interview, since impersonal interviewer behavior is more easily standardized than a more personal approach. . . . It is noteworthy that writers about schedule interviews are always fearful of the negative bias that the interviewer may introduce. . . . They say little or nothing about the positive contribution the . . . interviewer may make—e.g., using skill and charm to persuade respondents to stick with a schedule of questions that they may find thoroughly uncongenial.[51]

If there *is* a royal road to good data, we have greatest confidence in interviewers who report the greatest flexibility—those with a tendency to weave back and forth, now heading over toward the respondent with message of relatedness and diplomacy, now heading back over to the question where they speak with cool distance. Such interviewers confess that they vary their course according to how they read conditions—from respondent to respondent and from moment to moment.

When the question itself seems too cool or incongruous, the interviewer dissociates himself from it (and the anonymous souls who think up such things)—ever so slightly, as best he can, with language that leagues him subtly with the respondent. "I know—but we're almost through with this section now. Just one more question on this kind of thing." When he judges himself too close to the respondent, he steers away again, taking on the cool and distance of the question itself.

If researchers deem these practices unfortunate, they seem to us the best that can be done until the world itself is tidied up with more standardized respondents.[52]

On Interviews and Conversations

Why in the world are people willing to be interviewed? Beginning interviewers find that willingness something of a wonder, and precisely because they are doubtful (and grateful), they take careful note of the pleasures that respondents seem to find.[53] As human communication, interviews obviously have a different quality than ordinary dialogue, but interviewers discover that some of the differences actually commend the interview. For four reasons most commonly cited, an interview can *beat* just talking.

1. *Interested listening.* Good Listeners are noteworthy enough in our ordinary social life as to merit that particular label. Even conversations between close friends can take on something of the air of a friendly contest between two good talkers, neither of whom ever really finishes a thought, so lively is their dialogue of interruptions. Despite their initial doubt, interviewers generally come to be convinced that attentive listening really does reward the respondent for his time and talk. The following student records a very common discovery:

> It may be surprising, though I realize that it shouldn't be, to discover that most people really like to talk, especially about their opinions on social problems and family matters. Not only that: they especially like to be listened to. There really aren't so many occasions when one really has the feeling that he is being listened to, that his opinions really are important to the hearer. I don't mean just being quiet. I mean the kind of real paying attention— with the verbal and visual kinds of genuine interest. Interviewers are strangers, to be sure, but their genuine listening at least partially repays their respondents, I am now convinced.

This interviewer (as do most) has sloughed off the apologetic or guilty feeling that he is ruthlessly extracting opinions from the mine of the unsuspecting public.

2. *The personal and experiential.* Most conversation is generally pointed to the immediate present or the activity at hand. Talking gets grooved into certain channels. To embark on one's own life, plans, or feelings often requires a leisurely private occasion and friends who are indeed good listeners.

Public opinion surveys often do not provide any substantial portion of questions bearing on personal history. But some questions elicit personal reflection or bear on one's own unique past and present. The most poignant revelations often emerge when respondents ruminate about these pathways of their own lives, not when they consider questions bearing on sex or income or other matters that interviewers expect to be sensitive or revealing. One young man was witness to just such a moment of recaptured history by a thoughtful middle-aged woman:

> Do you know I have never really told *anyone* why I actually dropped out of school. I couldn't even tell my parents or talk about it at all with them. I'm glad my daughter is not the way I was—so fearful. Probably I was over-protected.
>
> I dropped out because I was afraid of a white face! The teacher had a booming voice and a white face and he scared me half to death. He was really a kind man and he tried his best to persuade me to finish and go on in journalism. He even had the principal talk to me and tell me that it was a shame for me not to finish. But it was his face!

The thoughtful black woman, now many years and understandings removed from her youthful timidities, was perhaps even inspired to this reflection by the *interviewer's* white face.

3. *The minimal costs.* Recapturing and expressing such personal feelings is not regularly facilitated in social situations, and neither is the free expression of even less personal attitudes and opinions. Social life generally requires a modicum of tact and caution, and we become sensibly chary of sounding off our opinions without checking around a bit. We generally pick out spots for "free expression"—where it will not antagonize people whose good will we require or jeopardize relationships we value.

Interviews offer such a spot. No one will spread the word; no one will be offended, as a rule; no one will require apology the next day. Even when questions do not bear very directly on personal matters, many respondents take advantage of this freedom to *pronounce* with impunity and hold forth on controversy without back talk.

She was bitter and caustic about many topics, laughing sarcastically before and after many questions, but she was always civil to me and often very warm and friendly. I'm not entirely sure why. I felt that it had to do with my listening to her accusations without flinching or arguing. She seemed to appreciate my noncommittal responses, and she proceeded with many angry, bitter views.

There can thus be some of the same privacy and freewheeling about one's own feelings that a therapeutic or social casework interview can provide. But surveys are generally somewhat more cost-free: the respondent is not being visited because he is a "case" or because he is considered in need of some help. He is being valued, even if briefly, for his individual experiences and views.

4. *Stimulation and new insight.* Questions of public opinion usually encourage reflection on old opinions and some formulation of new ideas—things the respondent has not thought much about before or at least not lately. In the margins of the questionnaire, one often finds a spontaneous comment of a respondent, "I could talk on a lot of things here for an hour," or, "Well, I've never thought about it exactly that way before. Let me think for a minute what I *do* think about that." It is something of a relief and a pleasure for interviewers when they accumulate evidence of respondents' pleasure in mental process itself:

> In the interview training they insisted that communication was actually enjoyable for respondents, but I was dubious until I heard a number of comments such as, "You know, this is all right! A guy never thinks of some of these things most of the time."

> This kind of reaction often came from bright respondents who, because of particular circumstances, had been forced to work at uninteresting jobs that provided them no mental stimulation. One respondent eagerly launched into a series of questions exclaiming, "This is just like being in school again." In a few cases, the dialogue became exciting for me too, and went a long way toward dispelling the sense of guilt I first felt at intruding upon a man's time and activities.

Interviews have uses for the respondent when they provide the kinds of psychic and intellectual stimulation that interviewers have reported. But interviews are put to many an unintended use as well. One charming respondent, a bon vivant in his twenties, thought so highly of the questionnaire that he begged the interviewer for an extra copy. He wanted it for a party that evening—"more fun than Monopoly," as he quipped. (The interviewer summoned all due professionalism and refused.) However insouciant the manner of the young man, it was probably quite a serious request. At least many people find that they would like to "try it out on friends," to see familiar people in the new perspective that they have just themselves considered.

Family members listening to the questions and answers not infrequently discover new things about their *own* respondent. At the end of one interview, the listening wife thanked the interviewer warmly: she never knew her husband's opinions on a lot of those things—it was so interesting! Sometimes family members will seize the moment for a discussion among themselves that they have never quite had. An interviewer reports being very moved by just such an exchange between a father and his college-age son:

> The son was present but it did not seem to change the respondent's attitude in answering. If anything, he voiced his determination that this was *his* interview and *his* opinion and he'd try to answer to the best of his ability. The father was a gentleman of the old school, very gracious and courteous; and his son, an only child, studying sociology in college, was also very gracious and mannerly.
>
> When the father gave his opinions on welfare, the son reacted, expressing surprise and irritation. The father spoke to him directly, without anger, just in a normal civilized manner: "Now, just keep quiet a minute and let me speak my piece. I don't think this is Generation Gap or anything: you just live in another world than the one I've lived in. I don't mean it as criticism of you or anything, but you have never had to earn money or pay for anything yourself. I've come up the hard way and I've had to work very hard to get the job I have, the house we own, the college education you're getting. It's my money that pays for welfare and ADC and crime and vandalism, and I'm plenty tired of all the taxes I have to pay. When you start paying your own way and doing your share, then you can talk. . . ."
>
> The son broke in, he too speaking without anger: "That's the trouble, Dad. All you people think of is the darn dollar. People are all human; they don't want your money. All they want is for you to help them by teaching them, getting right down to earth and digging with them, if necessary. Not just money. . . ."

They did not resolve the issue. "Remember," said the father, "it's still my dollar that buys the shovel—" and the son had to leave for an appointment. After he left, the father turned to the interviewer and told her that it was probably the frankest and most enlightening conversation he had had with his son.

We have only the interviewer's assurance that this was a tolerably unbiased interview; supervisors may read this and wince at the deviation from ideal interviewing conditions. But as the interviewer is sanguine about still other factors—her own ability to cope with such deviations; her pleasure in the experience that interviewing can offer people—she represents perhaps a final stage of confidence about her own role and the whole process. Indeed, this interviewer is an experienced professional, but it is a confidence that students attain as well:

> Now that the interviewing is all over, I realize that the whole business is a much more straightforward, nonmanipulative, two-way encounter than I had anticipated. For the most part, I was asking people questions that they wanted to answer, *enjoyed* answering. Not in every question, to be sure, and not in every case, but generally I was in the position of wanting to find out things that people wanted to say. It really wasn't much of a con game, after all.
>
> Wouldn't it be splendid if it should turn out that the good questions—the ones that respondents really liked answering—should be the ones that produced the best data? Never mind, I shall simply assume that that kind of Justice rules survey research as a whole!

A becoming sort of conviction for an interviewer, however untested by research.[54]

SUMMARY

Learning the Role

The beginning interviewer's sense of strain is much like the one to be expected of any professional trying to take on the demeanor expected of people in the role, but the interviewer must acquire a professional style without long practice, usually without role models on the spot, and without the symbolic cues that signal other people to play their role *vis-à-vis* the professional. It is thus much more self-taught. Of the two essential self-restraints—suppressing personal opinions and restraining expectations—the latter is more important and more difficult for the interviewer to achieve. Any of several procedures suggested by interviewers may be helpful in sensitizing them to the limited range and content of their own expectations and in enlarging their own mental storehouse of human diversity, thus avoiding the stereotyping of expectations. Discipline and self-control may be facilitated indirectly either by expressive reaction against respondents' views after hours, or by finding intellectual discovery in understanding the vantage point of all respondents including those who express opinions hostile to the interviewer's own. When interviewers become technically confident of the schedule, they can relax their efforts to manipulate their own personality so strongly and shift the focus away from themselves to the respondent. This enables them to concentrate on transcribing and understanding what the respondent means and, at the same time, to recover confidence and poise with which to adapt to unanticipated features of the interview setting.

Continuing Cross-pressures

Even after the interviewer has developed a professional style, the situation itself will continue to feature cross-pressures between the social demands for conversations and the scientific demands for inquiry. When respondents strain for information about the interviewer and his ideas, ordinarily the interviewer should and can defer such disclosures until the end of the structured schedule; but in certain rare instances, refusing to deal immediately with the respondent's demand can threaten the interview even more than candid discussion might. The strain toward relationship can be more difficult to resist because the interviewer, too, experiences this tendency toward personalism, as relief from mechanical delivery of questions, especially with respondents he finds particularly congenial. When questions prove peculiarly inappropriate to a given respondent's situation, there is probably no remedy better than bearing the incongruity with humor—with the respondent if need be. When there appears to be tragedy or trauma inherent in the situation, however, the interviewer is faced with the decision of deleting the question or even cutting off the whole interview. The distress may be a mild and passing thing—curable by a greater sensitivity and responsiveness in the interviewer's delivery or by adaptation of question-order (although the latter raises problems of standardization). Frank discussion of the rare but serious situation should be undertaken in training sessions so that interviewers can better distinguish mild discomfort from what could be real injury to the respondent.

Role Requirements in Conflict

Interviewers are required to be both technically standardized and interpersonally responsive to many different kinds of individuals—a blend of styles that is often contradictory enough to require special modes of compromise and strain. Beginners probably exaggerate the warm, diplomatic approach to the respondent, but some seasoned interviewers may become rather cool and impersonal—especially if researchers themselves tend to emphasize clerical efficiency more than the dynamics and demands of the human relationship. Interviewer morale can be enhanced by training and field procedures that provide some focus on the dramas of individual respondents and situations and facilitate interviewers as a group in maintaining close contact with each other and with the research staff.

Maneuvers in the Field

Refusals

The best defense against the disappointment and discouragement of refusals is a recognition that the rejection is usually an expression of the respondent's own fear or resistance, not a negative judgment on the interviewer's competence. Refusals reflecting anxiety about urban crime and resentment of salesmen appeared to have increased in recent Detroit Area Studies, but many people, initially reluctant, respond to the sheer chance of a second interviewer or the patient courtesy of the first.

Getting the Interview

Most often, interviewers have little information about the nature of the respondent's resistance beyond their own best hunch of the moment, and they report these judgments on the spot as the most serviceable: (1) making appointment times—repeatedly if necessary—that accommodate the respondent; (2) reassuring the respondent that the time required for the interview will at least partly reflect the degree of interest the questions have for him; (3) treating all incidental encounters with tact and courtesy— since some of the encounters will prove helpful in locating or even persuading the respondent; (4) projecting a confident, reassuring, and thus legitimizing manner; an air of apology or defensiveness about intruding on a person's time may create more suspicion than it allays; and (5) conveying a genuine interest in the selected respondent, one aspect of which is indirectly projected by the patient activity of locating and accommodating the respondent at the outset.

Cutting the Conversation

Traditional theory and training stress the interviewer's role in opening up communication, but interviewers, in practice, often have to cope with tactfully restricting the flow of reminiscence or irrelevance. Digressions can be shortened by interviewer cues of inattention or even dexterous interruption, but some rumination or reminiscence may be essential for the respondent's continued concentration, interest, and sense of the interviewer's acceptance.

The Neutral Probe

The interviewer is to "probe" when the respondent's answer is so vague or general that a third person, unaware of the respondent's personal context or the interaction of the moment, would find little meaning in it. This requires knowing well the research aim of the question and applying it to intelligent listening, answer by answer. Probing the "don't know" answers requires an instant judgment of the personal meaning of the answer (professed ignorance being only one of the possibilities). Such probing instructions are often imperfectly standardized, partly because survey researchers tend to show a certain ambivalence toward public nonopinion. Very often the "don't know" answers—especially the initial ones preceding a codable answer—are put to no research use at all. Interviewers may honor this practice by pushing respondents for some sort of substantive answer (but they will do so with considerable variation in the persistence with which they press), yielding data that are an uncertain mix of genuine and "instant" opinions. Instructions generally provide probe wordings designed to elicit more information without biasing the respondent's answer, as in "Could you tell me more about why you feel that way?" The interviewer who adheres too closely to these literal wordings may sound somewhat mechanical to respondents. The more freewheeling interpreter of the probe language tends to style it to the tone and mood of the respondent. Earlier literature on interviewing stressed the exchange of personal warmth and the interviewer's skill in rapport building somewhat more than current writing does. This new emphasis projects greater concern about interviewer bias and a greater interest in standardizing interviewer performance, but it may neglect some of the positive contributions that interviewer warmth and personalism make—in getting the interview in the first place and in holding it through some difficult spots. Very recent research indicates that personal and impersonal interviewer styles function differently according to the respondent's educational level. Generally we suspect that the most successful interviewers are flexible in the degree of personalism they project or respond to, varying their style from one situation to another in response to their judgment of the immediate interactive requirements of the respondent.

Interviews and Conversations

The interview can offer to the respondent values that may be scarce in much ordinary conversation: (1) attentive listening; (2) consideration of the personal and experiential; (3) expression of controversial opinions without risk of argument or disapproval; and (4) intellectual stimulation and insight—all of which beginning interviewers note with relief and satisfaction that respondents get something out of the exchange, too.

III
IN DISTRUST OF DATA

In Defense of the Respondent

Most professional interviewers do not move on to the analysis of data, as student-interviewers do: they pursue *minuteness,* well pleased with the closeup shots of particular persons. Most researchers do not take 10 to 20 interviews a year, despite interviewers' strong recommendations: they ply their fascination for fashioning aerial views of the *massive* social landscape and the generality of persons. The ultimate product is a cooperative, joint effort. The process of an actual interviewing season, however, is rarely without flashes of what could be called, at the very least, cordial distrust.

First, a lagging response rate will rouse the researcher to high anxiety, and for the interviewers this means that the pressure is on. If an interviewer's sympathy for the beleaguered researcher is predictably scant, this "P.S." on a recent questionnaire may explain it:

> I'm going home to recover with a good stiff martini! I just wish some of you people were out here today, having the kind of day *I've* had!

Second, the questionnaire itself will be seen in different lights. Researchers, having proudly fashioned the best possible instrument with the available time, money, and staff, will entrust it to interviewers to administer with the best possible sensitivity and intelligence. Interviewers, however, can be uncharitable. When a question does not go well, for instance, they will insist that it is unrealistic, awkward, or that it makes people puzzle or laugh. Researchers will know that that is nonsense: the question is the very bulwark of the study, and interviewers are stubbornly refusing to ask it properly.

If open debate never breaks out between the two camps, look to the good offices of a discreet field supervisor who hears much, says little, and keeps researchers and interviewers well away from each other. For each group, the instruments and angle of vision are different, as well as the pressures and problems. Some signs of struggle are inevitable.

The sign of the crossed sword is unmistakable in the Detroit Area Study —struggle is perhaps more openly expressed than in most survey research organizations. For one reason, student-interviewers know too much! As they participate in all phases of the construction and conduct of a survey, not only interviewing, they have a broader overview than interviewers generally do, with many opportunities to observe discrepancies between ideals and realities of practice. Furthermore, because they are using this experience in their own professional aspiration and development, their criticisms ring with a certain evangelism. Indeed, they take on something of the role of heretic—insiders, hopeful of reforming from within, eager to put their own improved stamp on traditional practice.[55] Looking at the field from the unique vantage point of interviewer-and-researcher, they can offer useful and sophisticated criticism.

The interviewer's own task and problems tend to make him an advocate for the respondent, more than a defender of information and ideas for social science. What will the respondent find reasonable to answer? How much time will he really be willing to spend? What will he answer freely, without embarrassment, without growing bored or hostile—without, indeed, showing the interviewer summarily to the door? Most important perhaps, what will he really *enjoy* because it is interesting to think about? These objectives may not necessarily comport perfectly with what the researcher wants to *know*. To be sure, interviewers can be counted on to be sometimes overconfident of their intimate knowledge of the total population, but their advocacy serves to nag the researcher back toward the reality of the persons under study. Interviewers will usually do their best, in pretesting, to simplify and clarify the language of questions and to argue for as sprightly a format as possible.

Pretesting the Language

A "pretest" can sound almost as if a question were simply *released* for a trial run and naturally came home a winner. As a matter of fact, many a question is cut to ribbons by the comments of interviewers and sent back for rehabilitation or retirement. It is a wise researcher who heedeth good counsel—when a whole group of interviewers carps and complains. If a question is wordy, unwieldy, difficult, or just plain hilarious to ask, interviewers are the first to know it. For example, this ponderous item appeared in a recent pretest of ours:

> Suppose you were working for a company where you could always be sure of having a job, but the chances of getting ahead were pretty poor. Then you were offered a job with a new company which would pay twice what you were earning, but there

> was a 50–50 chance that the company might go out of business. Do you think you would *almost certainly take* the job, *possibly take* it, or *not take* it?

After rehabilitation, the question read this way:

> In general, do you think a person would be better off taking a job that paid well but might not last—or a job which paid somewhat less but had greater security?

Less of a mouthful, surely.

Interviewers' criticisms in this case are doubtless an instance of what the Webbs had in mind:

> . . . the subordinate in any organization will yield richer veins of fact than the mind of the principal . . . not merely because the subordinate is usually less on his guard, and less severely conventional in his outlook. The essential superiority lies in the circumstance that the working foreman, managing clerk, or minor official is himself in continuous and intimate contact with the day-by-day activities of his organization; he is more aware than his employer is of the heterogeneity and changing character of the facts; and he is less likely to serve up dead generalization, in which all the living detail becomes a blurred mass, or is stereotyped into rigidly confined and perhaps obsolete categories.[56]

The Format of the Questionnaire

Some of the generalizations that researchers appear to apply in constructing questionnaires seem rather "dead" to interviewers. In published writing about survey methods, for instance, the issue of closed versus open-ended questions is only occasionally lively since there seem to be well-advertised advantages, disadvantages, and special uses for each type of format. But when interviewers begin to use a pretest questionnaire, the debate is likely to flare anew.

On the Failure of Questions. Researchers do not usually champion the open question. The practical problems are manifold. The open question burns up time prodigiously (and needless to say, the researcher is budget conscious). Constructing meaningful code categories from the welter of individual answers is exacting, artful, and costly. The actual coding of answers is predictably a good deal less reliable than that of closed questions and it tends to produce varied frames of reference, difficult to order along a single dimension. Empirical evidence to clinch the case is not abundant, but researchers veer toward closed questions for still another reason. As Richardson put it,

> . . . it seems likely that respondents of low intelligence, low socio-economic status, or low status in an organizational hierarchy may find it difficult to tolerate a preponderance of open questions, because they are unused to talking at length spontaneously, articulately, or coherently, or because they are uncomfortable in any unstructured situation, or because they feel that they are failing to grasp the interviewer's purpose, or for all these reasons.[57]

When he feels that there is a reasonable choice, the researcher is likely to opt for closing up the question, restricting the respondent to selecting his answer among stated alternatives. This certainly does economize on interviewer time and code-construction costs, but does it really address the problem that Richardson raises of respondent comprehension and articulateness? When an open question fails, the researcher (or his coder) faces, to be sure, what may prove to be an almost uncodable mess. But closing up the question may simply protect the researcher from learning that the respondent did not fully understand the question or its frame of reference. He has a check in a box, a number, a point on a scale—and it is *data,* regardless of what curious frame of reference or idiosyncratic mode of thought was actually triggered by the question during the interview.

When the closed question fails, it is the interviewer who is likely to know it and feel it. He is right there, absorbing the perplexity or the complaint of the respondent who chafes at the restriction of the forced choice:

> Why, I can't answer one way or the other. It's obviously both. Who makes up these crazy questions, anyway! No, I *said* put down *both.* Or nothing. How much longer does this go on?

If the interviewer at this point cannot open up the narrow channels of the choice (and pass the buck back to the researcher) he can at least try to share some of the pain. This interviewer's shaft—"He hated the closed questions; that's what I get for having an intelligent respondent!"—was surely not aimed at the Ignorant Public. Another interviewer's praise for his respondent is not without some delicious malice for the researcher: "Fantastic woman! Her insightful perception and intelligence certainly made mincemeat of some of the questions." [58] The hypothetical researcher, properly stung, would doubtless mutter: "An open question would have given us mincemeat in the first place, and how do you make analytical categories out of *that?*"

Polling with Procrustes

The format of the question itself is rarely an issue to interviewers when respondents seem to speak from their own experience or deliver genuine opinions. But interviewers tend to cavil at the constraints of the closed question when they feel that the questions do not capture the quality of the respondent's thought. One interviewer argues for many with the metaphor of Procrustes, the genial host of Greek mythology who made sure that his guests fit the bed (stretching the too-short and chopping off the too-long *guest*). With hypothetical questions, the interviewer felt herself stretching the respondent very thin indeed:

> If the person did not have any experience with the State Police or the FBI, we insisted that he imagine what he would do *if*. On other matters—lawyers, the courts—if he did not have a genuine opinion, we badgered him politely into getting one quick.

The interviewer was well aware that the purpose of these questions was to compare attitudes toward different levels of government, instead of to capture real experience, but that knowledge did not assuage her discomfort:

> This became a painful process. I probably did not ask some of the questions well because I had found them prickly during the pretest—they seemed to interfere with rapport—but I really think the questions themselves were even more at fault. Had they gone on a minute longer with one of my respondents, I surely would have been turned out: she was distressed by feeling uninformed and ignorant. Even less fluttery souls volunteered that they weren't very smart, probably shouldn't be interviewed, really didn't have any idea in the world; others exhibited restlessness and boredom. Most respondents seemed to think that I, the interviewer, probably *knew* the "answers" to these questions while they were being forced into displaying their ignorance.
>
> One doesn't have to over-identify with a respondent to feel uncomfortable at stretching him to fit the question!

In other closed questions, the same interviewer felt that she had to take up Procrustes' ax to chop off those respondents who "tended to display more acuity and intelligence than we wanted to know."

> They resisted the either/or alternative; they qualified their answers; they rejected the cliché or the stereotype. Many of my

respondents showed much greater information and sophistication than the question choices permitted, and not only the highly-educated respondents at that. When I asked one young woman the question on political efficacy, she said, "Well, I guess I'll agree that the average person can 'get what he wants'—as long as he doesn't *want* very much." She had no great stock of formal education, but I'd be hard-pressed to give a shrewder answer than that. Ha, I wonder how it will be coded.

Other respondents facing the interviewer's ax finally did choose between Agree and Disagree. "But the qualifications and reasons they gave quite neutralized the actual choice—though it's only the final choice that will show up as data."

Some of these final choices, however arbitrary they may seem to respondents and interviewers, will indeed be the final data, and analytically meaningful at that. We nevertheless suspect that it would be useful if researchers more often gathered data on the adequacy of closed questions. A judicious use of the "random probe" of closed questions is just such a feasible means.[59] Interviewers might also routinely record when the question seemed to be a poor fit—and whether the respondent was being stretched out or chopped off. It is just the sort of information that would be handy for analysis of the questionnaire itself and for systematic inquiry into the fit between people and surveys. Without such standardized procedures built into the questionnaire, interviewers are likely to vary in the degree that they press the issue, much as they vary in probing the "don't know" answers. Neither standardized interviewer performance nor more trenchant analysis of questions and their format can be expected if the matter is left to individual initiative.[60]

If respondents actually answer much the same way for both the open and closed versions of a question, there are surely compelling reasons for choosing the more economical form. There is indeed some evidence to the contrary, of course. For instance, in some elegant sleuthing by Back and Gergen, substantial numbers of respondents were found to change their open-ended answers when confronted with the alternatives of the closed version.[61] But even if closed and open answers are found to be entirely comparable, *interviewers are still likely to want some open questions.* Although they require the labor of long transcription, sensitive probing, and artful pacing of the conversation (no interviewer in his right mind would argue for a totally open schedule), interviewers will want a sprinkling: a few here and there, to loosen up the interaction, to allow the respondent some freedom to rummage around in his mind, and to provide a bit of variety to the interviewer.

Variety as Kindness

The critical ingredient is doubtless variety. When interviewers face the task of pacing the conversation, it certainly helps if the questions themselves provide the respondent some alternation between the crisp choice and more reflective answers; some questions that can be answered *without* a great deal of thought and others that invite considerable mulling. This is most importantly a matter of the match between the particular respondent's thought and the particular question's content, but the most interesting issues in the world can be dulled by too mechanical a format or wording.

Sheer *style* deserves more attention in survey research than it gets. Question writing is most often seen as the art of constructing an idea within a context that most people will find realistic, plausible, and neutral, cast in the language and frame of reference that most people will find clear. There seems to be a rather widespread faith that a question that is *good* by these criteria will also keep a respondent on the edge of his seat, giving his all for social science. (Perhaps better: that it does not matter whether the respondent is on the edge of his seat.)

There is doubt in the minds of many interviewers and a few researchers. In a recent article, Elisabeth Noelle-Neumann taxes researchers with biasing their data when they bore their respondents. First, she sounds quite like our most "humanistic" interviewers:

> There appears to be a general belief that avoidance of monotony in questionnaires is merely a matter of being kind to respondents; of unnecessary kindheartedness, to be more precise. It is surprising indeed how many researchers expect that the degree of monotony of an interview will not influence its results. It *will* influence the results because, after all, respondents are not machines but human beings, motivated in their attitudes and behavior by their likes and dislikes.[62]

But then, from her own extensive research experience, she offers evidence to buttress the impressionistic accounts of our interviewers. She finds that when respondents become actively engaged and interested in a question, the distribution of answers changes. In a controlled experiment, the figures for newspaper readership were 10 to 15 percent higher when the question required more activity from the respondent (answering verbally versus matching papers and reading-frequency with strips of paper); and there was even a small increase in readership when the newspaper questions were identical but one questionnaire was as a whole more "animated." (It is not entirely clear from the article that the second form of the question produced the more valid data, although one suspects that it did.)

The research issue remains rather open, and, indeed, Noelle-Neumann's basic argument is that there is a great need for evidence with which to construct "rules" for the wording of the structured questionnaire. Until much more systematic inquiry is brought to the art of questionnaire writing (not just single questions but the whole schedule), the interviewers' insistence on the respondent's right to variety seems to provide the best guide to practice. (Some of the sternest interviewers even add that boring respondents should be considered immoral!)

Interviewers contend that respondents do not enjoy any kind of question when it recurs in an unrelieved battery of exactly the same code categories or general format. The constant repetition of

> Do you agree or disagree?
> So would you say very good, somewhat good, not very good, or no good at all?

—over and over again, through some 20 or 30 questions, for example. Such arrangement of questions would seem to be such an obvious fault in "artistry" as to require no comment, but questionnaires of this kind are unfortunately not uncommon.

We are satisfied that variety is not merely a matter of "opening up" a few closed questions. While recently listening to some tape-recorded interviews, we were sufficiently struck by the dullness of the interaction as to become intrigued by the format of the schedule. We found that open questions constituted only 9 percent of the minimum number of questions that an "average" respondent would answer (generally a smaller proportion than in recent Detroit Area Study schedules). We chose another questionnaire for comparison, although we did not have taped interviews, because we ourselves, as hypothetical respondents, had found it particularly interesting to think about. The proportion of open questions was even smaller.

The second questionnaire offered content that was more experiential and personal, and thus doubtless had the edge in appeal, but the format itself had much more diversity. After a small batch of questions requiring Yes/No, Agree/Disagree, or five-point scales of one kind and another, there was a shift into another style of questioning: a list of words, choosing from a batch of things, matching this with that, and so on. Never in the course of the schedule was the interviewer faced with picking up one kind of question and hauling it along through 20 or 30 monotonous repetitions.

Although we cannot bring more evidence that boring respondents biases data, we *have* the data to defend the proposition that researchers must make their questionnaires interesting and artful to keep their *interviewers* interested. (Coders of our acquaintance say that the same goes for them!) Repetition is, of course, something of an occupational hazard for interviewers, even at best, so they would seem justified indeed in wanting variety in format *within* as well as *between* questionnaires.

The Bias of Rationality

The most skeptical interviewers, especially student-interviewers, are quick to note ways in which question-wording or format structures the social reality, even falsifying it. Other than the essential truism that the interpretation of results must be grounded in the actual questions asked, we do not have much data or theory to guide us in this area. There have been scattered experiments and quasi-experiments that indicate clearly that small variation in question wording affects percentage frequencies and even association among items.[63] But purely logical and experimental analyses of question wording, important though they are, miss certain problems that may be apparent only to the insightful interviewer. In the following paper, a thoughtful student reflects on the discrepancy between racial action she has experienced and racial attitudes she has "sampled." Her caveats would seem to have wider implication than race alone.[64]

> In the summer of 1966, Martin Luther King was marching in Chicago, and I had gone to see a demonstration of blacks in one of the lower-middle class suburbs. The blacks were well dressed, marching in single file, and were heavily guarded by rows of police. We watched on the "white" side of the road. The people here were not so clean-cut-looking as the demonstrators and some were quite dirty.
>
> The suburban whites were up in arms. Young teenage girls, with blond pigtails, of Polish descent, helped their parents and grandparents sling vulgar, ugly phrases at the blacks. They all laughed at their own insulting witticisms but they seemed in dead earnest. They reminded me of little boys watching a wounded sparrow trying to escape their cruel hands.
>
> At one point we could see hundreds of whites swarm into a central spot. We never learned what incident triggered their interest at that moment, but the next day's paper carried headline stories describing incidents involving 13 overturned and damaged cars, along with heavy rock-throwing on the part of the white brothers.

In the spring of 1968, while interviewing in Detroit suburbs, the interviewer finds the contrast amazing:

> My white respondents were so reasonable and calm and rational about their prejudice. Their views, heavily racist, were expressed without detectable hostility, really—in fact, in an almost emotionless manner. Thoughtful, reasonable, even if grammatically poor or structurally not too logical, nothing in their tone matched the heated reaction of the Polish neighborhood of 1966.

The interviewer realizes that her collection of Detroit respondents may not be representative; that the two communities may be quite different; and even that times may have changed in a scant two years. But what inspires her analytical curiosity is the interviewing situation itself, virtually all components of which she sees as operating to reduce emotion and intensify rationality. In the following five factors, she sees the cumulative force of the bias of rationality:

1. *The respondent is asked for his opinions not his feelings.* At the very outset, he is appealed to on an intellectualized level; he is expected to be at his thoughtful best.
2. *The emotionality of questions has been filtered out in pretesting.* We were concerned about exciting strong reactions in respondents. Fearful that such feelings might lead them to break off the interview, we tried to smooth out rough spots in content as well as form.
3. *There is formality in the very style of question-wording that reduces spontaneous expression.* Repetition of code categories ("Are you generally satisfied, somewhat satisfied, not at all satisfied?") creates some distance between the question and the respondent. Forced choice among closed alternatives does the same thing. I found my respondents stopping to think—not presumably about the nature of their own opinion as much as about the formal alternatives we were offering them. I realize that such formality is necessary for the standardization of answers and codes, but it also acts to reduce spontaneity and feeling and exaggerate cool rationality.
4. *The one-to-one interview setting excludes the force of normal interpersonal or group influence.* The kind of respondent who might well riot against blacks in response to others is not detected in the interview. For example, one of my woman respondents would doubtless never become aggressive against blacks by herself, but she might do so under the influence of her husband and daughters. She would certainly think what her husband told her to think (and in fact I had a good deal of trouble con-

vincing the rest of the family that they could not answer questions for her; initially, she felt incapable of answering and they seemed to agree with her estimate). In this lady's case, on this particular set of attitudes, it would have been of greater predictive value to get the attitudes of the husband and daughters.

The interviewer's final point seems to us the most trenchant criticism:

5. *The tone of the interviewer herself is ultrareasonable.* One of the ways in which we are to "minimize bias" is to ask questions in a neutral tone of voice, reasonable, matter-of-fact: utterly unlike even a discussion on race that friends or neighbors might have, much less the highly charged scene of a racial demonstration of taunts, rocks, and mob action. It seems to me that all our efforts to minimize the influence of others, including the interviewer, really conspire to extinguish one kind of bias while generating another—the bias of rationality.

The interviewer's analysis (proceeding well beyond the familiar observation of the poor fit between attitudes and behaviors) raises fundamental questions about the traditional conduct of the survey interview. As David Riesman put it some time ago, we bring a "cool methodology" even to "hot" topics.[65] Professionals in the field are well aware that opinion survey does not explore the conditions of behavior, nor (more importantly here) does it illuminate human attitudes in all their richness—their situational determinants and variability, their complex and even contradictory nature. Indeed, the canons of present practice—the one-to-one setting, the formalized questions, and the supportive but neutral interviewer—tend to militate against such explorations.

There has been little experimental tinkering with conventional practice for the very good reasons that the practical obstacles are formidable and the theoretical guidelines thin. The training labors involved in Marquis et al.'s experiment with "reinforcement" comments by interviewers are sobering reminders of the practical costs.[66] Many researchers doubtless feel, along with Ithiel de Sola Pool, that the most basic and interesting data are imbedded in the "interpersonal dynamics of the interview" and the ways in which people handle opinions. As he says, "If we learn enough about the characteristics of our instrument then our most valid measures will come from observing what happens as we manipulate it." [67] But such experimental manipulation—costly and complex—warrants more compelling theoretical direction that is current in the field to date.

It would seem that Leo Bogart's 1967 address still stands as a basic challenge:

Now it says here, "In a cheerful tone, continue with Question 44B."

> The prevailing model . . . [of a single opinion] . . . has the
> virtue of great simplicity but it makes no sense, because con-
> flicting and contradictory opinions may be held simultaneously
> and because they constantly jostle each other for dominance. . . .
>
> It has taken the opinion research profession a third of a century
> to gain acceptance for the principle of systematic sampling. It
> may take the next third to dispel the illusion that descriptive
> measures of public opinion represent the "real thing," and to
> establish that our primary task is to understand how opinions
> come to be held at all, and how they evolve and change.[68]

For ingenious researchers—with sufficiently captious interviewers—that
may be time enough.

Unpainting the Pictures

The interview was not even half over when a young man was suddenly
struck: "Hey, if you put that all together, it's *me!*" Presumably the tactful
interviewer (well pleased by the compliment, we trust) did *not* respond,

"Don't be silly—nobody's going to put you all together. They're going to take you all apart!" But that fate is in store.

The interviewer and the respondent have cooperated painstakingly in fashioning an individual portrait, but only the interviewer will preserve that image. From now on, the picture of the respondent will be taken apart, in a kind of perverse *unpainting to number*.

The researcher (or his coders) will take the interview and scrub and bleach out the color, a bit at a time:

> How much education?—just about as much as I could stand. That high school graduation day was the happiest day of my life, and don't think the teachers weren't happy too! They thought they'd never get rid of me.

How much education?—*12*. All manner of opinions and feelings will be ruthlessly stripped down. If the young man should want his son to be *like him* in

> trying to be nice to people, helping them out when they need a five or a ten and you can wait until payday. Maybe I mean not being too tightfisted when you've got a little extra and other people are in trouble . . .

the coder will doubtless decide that he really means "5—ethical concerns." Little by little, the picture will be scraped down, piled up most unceremoniously with the numbers of other people, and fed into the maw of the computer.

For any interviewer given to brooding, there is special pain in knowing about the unpainting proclivities of survey researchers. The knowledge can reduce an interviewer's care and exactness. (And that will worry a brooding investigator. Unless the interviewer gets it all down exactly, the respondent will be unpainted down to the *wrong* number!) At the very least, it can induce a special skepticism about survey results.

Interviewers may be doubtful because their set of respondents is simply not representative of the total sample. The statistical rarities, after all, are precisely the people who capture the interviewer's imagination: the sprightliness of the elderly person who champions social change and youthful rebellion, the wonderful toughness of the middle-aged housewife who throws down her garden tool to take out in hot pursuit of the purse snatcher, the stern advocate of law and order who has spent most of his young life in reform schools and prisons, the graying police officer who ardently advocates radical reform of the department. ("How could he do that to me!" laments the student-interviewer who has been active in radical politics. "I may not have a stereotype left!") But, more generally, interviewers know that the analysis of large numbers sheers off the unique particularity of individual respondents, and, by temperament and training, they are less fascinated by the trends and relationships of aggregate data than they are by the drama and color of live individuals.

SUMMARY

In Defense of the Respondent

Because of the nature of their own task, interviewers tend to criticize questionnaires from the standpoint of the respondent's reaction—his comprehension, interest, and pleasure in answering questions. They argue that most respondents require at least a few open-ended questions—to loosen up the dialogue if nothing else; and some variety in the language and format of closed questions—to maintain the respondent's interest and active participation. Interviewers need such features of questionnaire style for their own sake, as well, to mitigate some of the monotony inherent in administering the same questionnaire to many respondents. We would do well to gather systematic data more often on the common complaint that closed questions render very imperfectly certain respondents' thought and generate considerable respondent dissatisfaction. Interviewers are obviously less knowledgeable about the researchers' problems—for example, the challenge that open questions can pose at the time of code construction and data analysis—but such criticisms from the field are ordinarily worth the researcher's consideration, especially when there is fair consensus among interviewers.

The Bias of Rationality

If the researcher succeeds in insulating the interview from various kinds of bias, especially bias of the interviewer, he may well generate another form of influence that overintellectualizes and formalizes the interaction. In its basic design, the questionnaire elicits a respondent's intellectualized opinions more than his emotional reactions. Both by content and standardized format, emotionality and spontaneity are attenuated. As a rule, the situation is structured to protect the respondent from the interpersonal influence of those who ordinarily affect his attitude and behavior, and from the influence of the interviewer as well, whose prescribed neutrality further enhances the reasonable tone of the whole interchange. Researchers are not unaware of these limitations or the fact that opinion research has not yet developed many modes by which to study the complexity of human attitudes or the conditions under which they arise, develop, and change. But experimental modes for undertaking such study are costly from a practical standpoint; from a theoretical standpoint formulations are not very clear. For the most part, both obstacles serve to maintain current practice intact while the challenge to expand experiment remains relevant as well.

IV
IN PRAISE

We will praise famous interviewers no longer. A feisty lot they are, after all—full of contention in favor of respondents, full of reforms for the researchers, and supremely confident that their own "rich veins of fact" should edify the principals of any research organization. They have had their due. We reserve this final praise for the process of interviewing itself.

In the conduct of the Detroit Area Studies, we lack a major personnel problem of survey research organizations. Because we do not recruit interviewers, we devise no procedures to detect the applicants of greatest promise—we take what we get: graduate students headed toward careers in social science, required along the way to take a survey research practicum and thus obliged to interview. A few find it distasteful. Most find in it some sort of important learning experience. Whether or not this sense of discovery makes people better interviewers, we have come to be persuaded of the reverse moral: that interviewing makes for more capable—more insightful, even more compassionate—people.

Effective interviewing requires one person to take on the behavior that facilitates another person's expression of ideas and feelings. Adopting the superficial manner of sympathetic listening often induces the process of actually listening sympathetically. The dramatic interpersonal impact of the interviewer's own personality is diluted. He actually meets another human being on his own ground because the clash of personal styles or the interplay of negative first impressions or hostilities is muted or even excluded by the listening role of the interviewer. As one student expresses the process,

> Ordinarily I feel just as unfriendly toward the sort of people I interviewed—Middle Class Respectables—as they do to me, a bearded college student. If we met under most circumstances, we would have little to say to each other, and our respective stereotypes and assumed hostilities would reinforce each other.

John Madge sees in this suspension of one's own personality a "powerful human experience which leaves its mark on those who have practiced

79

"I pray thee, then, write me as one who loves his fellow men."

it." [69] We think that "mark" is the print of particular moments and individual persons—the sample of lives being lived. In ordinary social life, most of us listen to another while engaging in a simultaneous "presentation of the self." If this is not always the stage for the playing out of our "respective stereotypes and assumed hostilities," it is at least a two-person drama in which each person's reception of the other is counteracted by his need to generate active social behavior. The presentation of the interviewer's self is subordinated to the job of learning about another person, ideally helping him to express himself. The interviewer can thus learn things about other people—trivial, crucial, and irrelevant alike—that the press of his own personality in an ordinary conversation will often exclude. Interviewers remember some of their respondents almost in the fashion of a fond reader's remembrance of a David Copperfield or a Clarissa Dalloway: limned by artful characterization; uncomplicated by our own real-life relationships to them; fully attended.

We used to be convinced that interviewing should be a required course for *all* students. In the course of writing this book, however, we have come to consider that it might be a citizen responsibility—something like jury duty, perhaps. But that is surely going too far: there should probably be a continuing division of labor between respondents and interviewers. After all, do you find that more things "happen" to you than to other people? Do your friends listen to you silently enthralled? Do you shine at parties as raconteur? You may need something with a little more dazzle than interviewing.

On the other hand, as you rummage in your mind right now, do you find that you have all kinds of miscellaneous "data" about your friends—where they grew up, where their families came from, which grandfather was the Black Sheep? When a stranger sits next to you on a plane, do you usually get off knowing where he works, whether he's married, how many children he has, and how he feels about issues of the moment? (And what has that stranger learned about you?) You have probably been interviewing for years.

In order to do so for pay and professionalism, only a few additional tastes should be cultivated: a pleasure in hiking on pavement in all weather; a delight in "lousy coffee served on greasy counters;" a taste for long hours of speedy transcription; and, very probably, a sturdy distrust for all Authority, by which to pursue respondents—and instruct researchers.

V
ON FURTHER INSTRUCTION

Advice to interviewers is sprinkled widely in social science literature but sometimes rather thinly: it consists of a few pages on ideal practice, suggesting little of the rigors of the field or the reality of respondents. Another type of writing examines some instance or other of interviewer "bias" with all the earnestness of a housewife pursuing the last speck of domestic dust. The writings that follow are a selection that we have found richer—for the scope of research interest, for the ingeniousness of analysis, for the range of experience or the quality of reflectiveness. We have included some selections from the tradition of "free" interviewing with the unstructured schedule, writing that is not generally seen as very germane to the problems of constructing or conducting the standardized schedule of survey research. We have done so precisely because we think there is some overlap of problems and possibilities—at the very least for understanding the human situation in the interview and for entertaining new possibilities for systematic experiment. Certain researchers remain fascinated by the perils and delights of interviewing the ruggedly unique individual on the other side of the schedule, whatever form that interview takes, and their insights are rarely without some implication or application for survey research. For more extensive bibliography, see Dexter (1), Gorden (2), and Cannell and Kahn (9).

(1) Lewis Anthony Dexter, *Elite and Specialized Interviewing,* Evanston, Ill., Northwestern University Press, 1970. Reflections on elite interviewing seen in the light of published findings and his own revisions in practice along the way. The bibliography, largely annotated, is very interesting.

(2) Raymond L. Gorden, *Interviewing: Strategy, Techniques, and Tactics,* Homewood, Ill., The Dorsey Press, 1969. The bibliography is an extensive one, although not annotated.

I. Persons and Places

(3) Oriana Fallaci, *The Egotists: Sixteen Surprising Interviews,* Chicago, Henry Regnery Co., 1968. Free interviewing of celebrities. Despite the title, Fallaci is fond of most of her respondents but reserves a marvelous acerbity for the few overwhelmed by their own importance. Dangerous reading: just the sort of superb condensations of personality that could lead the aspiring social scientist to take up journalism or the novel.

(4) Daniel Lerner, "Interviewing Frenchmen," *American Journal of Sociology, 62* (2), September 1956, 187–194. Lerner finds evidence of "French national character" first in his respondents' initial resistance to being interviewed at all and then in their great volubility once they agreed. Lively with the local color of the respondents and with insights into the role of the interviewer.

(5) David Riesman, *Faces in the Crowd: Individual Studies in Character and Politics,* in collaboration with Nathan Glazer, New Haven, Yale University Press, 1952. A set of portraits generated by "holistic" analysis of interviews. The cast of questions and interpretations is a good deal more psychological than the general run of survey research, but the introductory chapter is nevertheless a valuable set of reflections on interviewing.

II. The Role of the Interviewer

(6) Kurt W. Back, Reuben Hill, and J. Mayone Stycos, "Interviewer Effect on Scale Reproducibility," *American Sociological Review, 20* (4), August 1955, 443–446. Interviewers were found to perform well on either conscientious completion of the questions *or* on the understanding of questions—not on both. Interviewers tended to wish more information on the very kind of task in which they were already the more skilled.

(7) Kurt W. Back and J. Mayone Stycos, *The Survey Under Unusual Conditions,* Monograph No. 1, Ithaca, New York, The Society for Applied Anthropology, Cornell University, 1959. Excellent material on the selection, training, and evaluation of interviewers in a study conducted in Jamaica, but with considerable application for the U.S. setting (especially with regard to researchers' sensitivity to interviewer morale).

(8) Charles H. Backstrom and Gerald D. Hursh, *Survey Research,* Evanston, Ill., Northwestern University Press, 1963. A crisp set of interviewer-training instructions that are useful if brief.

(9) Charles F. Cannell and Robert L. Kahn, "Interviewing," in Gardner Lindzey and Elliot Aronson, *The Handbook of Social Psychology,* 2nd ed., Vol. 2, Reading, Mass., Addison-Wesley Publishing Co., 1968, pp. 526–595. Cannell and his associates at the Survey Research Center have been in the forefront of continuing experiment on the interview. See also (17), (31), (32), (39), and (41). This chapter is a very valuable review of research and recommendations on validity, sources of bias, question-construction, respondent motivation, and interviewer training and selection. On selection: there seem to be no "characteristics which differentiate 'born interviewers' from the rest of the population," although measures of interpersonal sensitivity seem the best bet so far. On training: research has turned up no compelling guides to the most effective practices—the providing of opportunities for practice seems to be that aspect worthy of most stress. The bibliography, while not annotated, incorporates many useful references.

(10) Lewis Anthony Dexter, "The Good Will of Important People: More on the Jeopardy of the Interview," *Public Opinion Quarterly, 28* (4), Winter 1964, 556–563. Concern with abusing time and confidence of members of "elite" samples is of relevance for beginners doing practice interviews, as well as students working with academic samples. Examples of the violation of anonymity are sobering—worth stressing for all kinds of interviewing.

(11) Barbara Snell Dohrenwend, "An Experimental Study of Payments to Respondents," *Public Opinion Quarterly, 34* (4), Winter 1970–71, 621–624. An offer of $5 affected response rate very little. "To improve completion rates in general population surveys, we should put our money elsewhere." Debate on such utilities continues in subsequent issues.

(12) Barbara Snell Dohrenwend, John Colombotos, and Bruce P. Dohrenwend, "Social Distance and Interviewer Effects," *Public Opinion Quarterly, 32* (3), Fall 1968, 410–422. A model of interview interaction, in which the probability of interviewer bias increases as there is either too much social distance or too little. The interviewer's own attitudes will have greater impact when the social distance perceived by the respondent is small; personal effect will be small if social distance provides greater impact.

(13) Kathrine S. French, "Research Interviewers in a Medical Setting: Roles and Social Systems," *Human Organization, 21* (3), Fall 1962, 219–224. "Lay interviewers" with at least two years of college were found to be more effective as research interviewers in a hospital set-

ting than nurses (who remained concerned with patient care) or social workers (who continued to write elaborate, irrelevant case-histories).

(14) Lester Guest, "A New Training Method for Opinion Interviewers," *Public Opinion Quarterly, 18* (3), Fall 1954, 287–299. Experimental evidence that practice in coding during the training period is even more effective for reducing interviewers' errors than practice in interviewing.

(15) Herbert H. Hyman, *Interviewing in Social Research,* Chicago, University of Chicago Press, 1954. Classic in experimental inquiry and compilation of research into sources of bias operating in the interview, as well as reformulation of theoretical and practical considerations. Evidence that the interviewer's own ideology—the culprit in much writing prior to Hyman—is less powerful in biasing the respondent than the interviewer's expectations and stereotyping of respondents. The reflections of experienced interviewers, very interesting in their own right, provided the basis for Hyman's reexaminations. The interviewers whose habitual style was personable *but* task oriented, rather than highly involved with the personal life of the respondent, seemed to bring back the most confidence-inspiring data.

(16) Buford H. Junker, *Field Work: An Introduction to the Social Sciences,* Chicago, University of Chicago Press, 1960. Although the field work here is that of participant-observers, Chapter 5 records experiences of students whose problems and insights are very germane to survey research. The introduction by Everett C. Hughes is lively and candid.

(17) Robert L. Kahn and Charles F. Cannell, *The Dynamics of Interviewing,* New York, Wiley, 1957. Especially valuable for its transcripts and critiques of actual interviews. Points out the lack of relevant training in fields that routinely depend on interviewing (e.g., medicine). Useful discussion of kinds of interviews and theory of respondent motivation, as well as bias and probing.

(18) S. M. Miller, "The Participant-Observer and Over-Rapport," *American Sociological Review, 17* (1), February 1952, 97–99. Miller's early close relationship with union leaders precluded his asking them certain questions that would have been seen as antagonistic, and foreclosed the kind of contact with the rank-and-file that would have illuminated *their* view of problems.

(19) James E. Myers, "Unleashing the Untrained: Some Observations on Student Ethnographers," *Human Organization, 28* (2), Summer

1969, 155–159. Amusing—and alarming—account of students' research enterprises in which they tended to violate the canon preserving subjects' anonymity.

(20) Stephen A. Richardson, Barbara Dohrenwend, and David Klein, *Interviewing: Its Forms and Functions,* New York, Basic Books, 1965. Authors have abstracted the details of their rich interviewing experience and experiment a little severely for the general reader who may wish for more local color, but the analysis is rich and useful, especially of the basic components and interaction of the interview. Questions the usual assumption that directiveness is unpleasant for the respondent; explores the importance of congeniality and spontaneity; holds up to examination the orthodoxies of theorists and the naive self-reporting of field workers.

(21) Donald F. Roy, "The Role of the Researcher in the Study of Social Conflict: A Theory of Protective Distortion of Response," *Human Organization, 24* (3), Fall 1965, 262–271. The attempt to study social conflict as a participant-observer came to complete grief, as Roy found that without respondents who would play *their* role, he was like a Romeo without a Juliet. Relevant to survey interviewing as a solace—makes it look easier.

(22) Michael J. Shapiro, "Discovering Interviewer Bias in Open-Ended Survey Responses," *Public Opinion Quarterly, 34* (3), Fall 1970, 412–415. What looks at first like variation in respondent "verbosity" appears to be variation in probing: more aggressive interviewers elicited more items.

(23) Andrzej Sicinski, " 'Don't Know' Answers on Cross-National Surveys," *Public Opinion Quarterly, 34* (1), Spring 1970, 126–129. Across-the-board comparisons of national groups are oversimplified and risky; comparisons of similar groups—for instance, occupational groups—within each nation are probably more meaningful. An initial comparison that showed Norwegians had more information than Poles or French was reanalyzed to show that Norwegians were more willing to guess than to admit ignorance.

(24) J. Mayone Stycos, "Proceedings of the American Association for Public Opinion Research," *Public Opinion Quarterly, 18* (4), Winter 1954–1955, 450–453. Brief excerpts of Stycos' experiences in underdeveloped countries.

(25) Survey Research Center, *Interviewer's Manual,* Ann Arbor, Institute for Social Research, University of Michigan, 1969. A manual of instruction used by a major survey organization which incorporates many useful suggestions.

(26) Carol H. Weiss, "Interaction in the Research Interview: The Effects

of Rapport on Response," *Proceedings of the Social Statistics Section,* American Statistical Association, 1970, pp. 17–20. Recent concern and conflicting findings on whether rapport biases respondents seen in the context of fuzzy, noncomparable measures. Weiss speculates nevertheless that rapport has been overvalued and suggests that interviewers who "listen attentively and show that they understand and value the answers they receive are building as much rapport as they need."

(27) William Foote Whyte, "Interviewing in Field Research," in Richard N. Adams and Jack J. Preiss, *Human Organization Research,* Homewood, Ill., The Dorsey Press, 1960, pp. 352–373. Whyte is one of the few who testify to the interviewers' need to learn how to interrupt gracefully. Includes some useful summarizing of Richardson's work.

III. In Distrust of Data

(28) Kurt W. Back and Kenneth J. Gergen, "Idea Orientation and Ingratiation in the Interview: A Dynamic Model of Response Bias," *Proceedings of the Social Statistics Section,* American Statistical Association, 1963, pp. 284–288. Respondent's answers are seen as moves in two games that he tries to play simultaneously: information-giving game (the payoffs increase the more he can express his views) and ingratiation game (the payoffs increase as he makes a better impression on the interviewer). Ingenious secondary analysis showing large number of respondents playing ingratiation game.

(29) Howard S. Becker, "A Note on Interviewing Tactics," *Human Organization, 12* (4), Winter 1954, 31–32. To elicit more frankness from Chicago schoolteachers in unstructured interviewing, Becker found he could be tough—play dumb, look skeptical, and move always to the concrete level.

(30) Leo Bogart, "No Opinion, Don't know, and Maybe No Answer," *Public Opinion Quarterly, 31* (3), Fall 1967, 331–345. A challenge to the profession to set about trying to understand "our primary task . . . how opinions come to be held at all, and how they evolve and change."

(31) Charles F. Cannell, Kent H. Marquis, and Andre Laurent, *A Summary of Research Studies of Interviewing Methodology,* Ann Arbor, Survey Research Center, University of Michigan, 1971.

(32) Charles F. Cannell and Sally Robison, "Analysis of Individual Questions," in John B. Lansing, Stephen B. Withey and Arthur C. Wolfe, *Working Papers in Survey Research in Poverty Areas,* Ann

Arbor, Institute for Social Research, University of Michigan, 1971.

(33) Philip E. Converse, "Attitudes and Non-Attitudes: Continuation of a Dialogue," in *The Quantitative Analysis of Social Problems,* edited by Edward R. Tufte, Reading, Mass., Addison-Wesley Publishing Co., 1970, pp. 168–189. Certain apparent changes in opinion over time point to the instability of "nonattitudes" rather than actual changes—generated because surveys assume that respondents are a "vibrant bundle of attitudes" on a great range of topics. The centrality of a given issue could be measured by assessing the store of information that the respondent holds on that topic.

(34) Lewis Anthony Dexter, "Role Relationships and Conceptions of Neutrality in Interviewing," *American Journal of Sociology, 62* (2), September 1956, 153–157. Unstructured interview setting. When interviewing businessmen, Dexter was interpreted as a liberal academic hostile to business interests unless he actually prepared himself to see and feel the reality as his respondents did, using language that would communicate that sympathy. Interviewer facing the problem of whose *side* he will be neutral on.

(35) Barbara Snell Dohrenwend, "Some Effects of Open and Closed Questions on Respondents' Answers," *Human Organization, 24* (2), Summer 1965, 175–184. Evidence in support of closed questions, for their greater efficiency in keeping respondents on the track, with at least comparable validity and depth. Open questions are seen as more useful for special circumstances such as measuring salience, also when time-pressures preclude sufficient pretesting of closed wording.

(36) Barbara Snell Dohrenwend, "An Experimental Study of Directive Interviewing," *Public Opinion Quarterly, 34* (1), Spring 1970, 117–125. Examines notion that directive questions will bias respondents, concluding that they can be used to increase reporting of controversial behavior without running risk of inducing false over-reporting.

(37) Kenneth J. Gergen and Kurt W. Back, "Communication in the Interview and the Disengaged Respondent," *Public Opinion Quarterly, 30* (3), Fall 1966, 385–398. The "disengagement" theory of aging generally confirmed by the finding that the percentage of "no opinion" was greater in the over-60 group than in the middle aged, and greater in the middle aged than in the young. "If . . . differences in the degree of opinionation between respondents are relevant, the interviewer who accepts 'no opinion' responses will obtain regular differences according to age. The value of accepting or re-

jecting no opinion responses depends, therefore, on the interpretation and the purpose of the survey."

(38) Edith Fein, "Inner-City Interviewing: Some Perspectives," *Public Opinion Quarterly, 34* (4), Winter 1970–1971, 625–629. From her own interviewing experiences, Fein argues that most survey research projects an unwitting bias that devalues lower-class respondents, who indeed generalize but about different things in different terms than do those who have proceeded through the mainstream of American education.

(39) Ramon Henson, Charles F. Cannell, and Sally Lawson, *Effects of Interviewer Style and Question Form on Reporting of Automobile Accidents,* Ann Arbor, Survey Research Center, University of Michigan, 1973. The effectiveness of variation in interviewer style (personal versus impersonal) and question form (brief versus redundant) in eliciting recall of factual events is associated with the educational level of the respondent. Task orientation is posited to be the critical motivation—diminished in persons of higher education when the *personal* style apparently communicates acceptance of an appropriate answer (even if not factually complete) and increased in persons of lower education presumably because positive feedback provides encouragement and reduces anxiety. The more *impersonal* interviewer produces data of greater validity in the former group.

(40) Paul F. Lazarsfeld, "The Controversy over Detailed Interviews: An Offer for Negotiation," *Public Opinion Quarterly, 8* (1), Spring 1944, 38–60. The classic on the uses of closed and open questions. Lazarsfeld argues that of the six main functions for open questions, four can be carried by closed questions. (The two exceptions: finding influences for an opinion and clarifying relationships.) Choices must always be framed in terms of specific research objectives.

(41) Kent H. Marquis, Charles F. Cannell, and Andre Laurent, *Effects of Reinforcement, Question Length, and Reinterviews on Reporting Health Events in Household Interviews,* Ann Arbor, Survey Research Center, 1971. Different interviewing procedures show various effects by educational level of the respondent; for example, for individuals without high school education, interviewer reinforcement aided accuracy of reporting; long questions and reinterviews reduced it.

(42) Herbert McClosky, *Political Inquiry: The Nature and Uses of Survey Research,* New York, MacMillan Co., 1969. See especially pp. 57–63 on limitations of surveys, including a crisp treatment of usual criticisms. For example, should not social science study the "whole

man?" "Impossible to understand any man, much less a group of men, all at once and in his (or their) entirety." Science is not rigidly quantitative; only more precise than our ordinary use of "some" or "most."

(43) Elisabeth Noelle-Neumann, "Wanted: Rules for Wording Structured Questionnaires," *Public Opinion Quarterly, 34* (2), Summer 1970, 191–201. Evidence that avoiding monotony is a condition for improving validity. Underreporting is interpreted as arising from a question form that did not elicit respondents' active interest and participation. Also interesting—and various—results from two forms of a closed question.

(44) Stanley Payne, *The Art of Asking Questions,* Princeton, Princeton University Press, 1951. "Asking" in this case means writing. Deceptively simple guide, containing much useful information, even for experienced researchers. A "Checklist of 100 Considerations" condenses much useful material. A chapter likely to appeal to interviewers (subtitled "A Sermon on the Care and Treatment of Respondents") ends, "Putting words in the respondent's mouth is one of the worst things we can do, especially when we have obtained the interview in the first place on the basis that we would not try to sell him *anything.*" Chapter 8 shows variation in answers by question form.

(45) Ithiel de Sola Pool, "A Critique of the 20th Anniversary Issue," *Public Opinion Quarterly, 21* (1), Spring 1957, 190–198. The view that the emphasis should be on the dynamic content of the interview, "an interpersonal drama with a developing plot," in which "opinions may often be better viewed as strategies in a game than as doctrines in a credo" is suggestive of Back and Gergen's analysis (28). An interesting critique of the assumption that we can somehow "get rid of interpersonal effects so as to get at the truth which would be there if the interpersonal character of the interview didn't interfere."

(46) David Riesman and Nathan Glazer, "The Meaning of Opinion," *Public Opinion Quarterly, 12* (4), Winter 1948–1949, 633–648. An early article that has lost little of its intellectual luster, although the typologies of American character are no longer in the limelight. Analysis of assumptions undergirding survey research, that people actually *do* and thus *should* have a stock of opinions on issues covered by the media. Polling is seen as a form of culture that facilitates communication up and down the social hierarchy, reinforcing the democratic myth that decision-making elites are truly sensitive to mass opinion.

(47) David Riesman and Mark Benney, "The Sociology of the Interview," (1955) in Riesman, *Abundance for What? And Other Essays,* Garden City, New York, Doubleday and Co., Inc., 1964, pp. 517–539. A history of the interview as a research and cultural form. Contemporary polling seen in terms of mass communication, democratization of language and concepts (which tend to tongue-tie the more highly educated respondents), the shift to "rapport," and the personal accumulation of opinions like any other consumer product.

(48) Howard Schuman, "The Random Probe: A Technique for Evaluating the Validity of Closed Questions," *American Sociological Review, 31* (2), April 1966, 218–222. A procedure for probing a random sample of closed questions to clarify the intention, reasons, and frame of reference of the answer. (With this procedure, we have detected questions that were confusing or misunderstood.)

(49) Howard Schuman and Jean M. Converse, "The Effects of Black and White Interviewers on Black Reponses in 1968," *Public Opinion Quarterly, 35* (1), Spring 1971, 44–68. A recent experiment in which race of interviewer is systematically varied for black respondents. Effects on type of question and type of respondent are examined, and difficult issues of validity are raised but not settled.

(50) A. Strauss and L. Schatzman, "Cross-Class Interviewing: An Analysis of Interaction and Communicative Styles," *Human Organization, 14* (2), Summer 1955, 28–31. A social class interpretation of differential ability in respondents to generalize, to adopt the frame of reference of another, and to articulate experience in ways communicable to persons unfamiliar with the immediate community. Riesman, in "The Sociology of the Interview" (46), draws different conclusions from the same data.

(51) Philip Taietz, "Conflicting Group Norms and the 'Third' Person in the Interview," *American Journal of Sociology, 68* (1), July 1962, 97–104. One of the few studies using the interview setting as a variable. When older Dutch adults were asked how they felt about their grown children living with them, their answers varied systematically with the presence of the spouse and of children. Interestingly, Taietz analyzes the effect of the college-age interviewer as similar to the effect of the children themselves.

IV. In Praise

(52) June Sachar Ehrlich and David Riesman, "Age and Authority in the Interview," *Public Opinion Quarterly, 25* (1), Spring 1961, 39–56.

The interviewer with a "flexible" personal style does not seem to inject bias by age, even when she is middle-aged and the respondent is young. Interviewers older than mid-fifties, however, seem to be seen by young respondents as authority figures regardless of their personality characteristics.

(53) John Madge, *The Tools of Social Science,* London, Longmans, Green, and Co., 1953. The overview of social science methods is worth reading in entirety, but see especially Chapter 4 on the interview, which classifies the major types, discusses the relevant skills, and projects a rich appreciation of the human experience.

(54) David Riesman, "Some Observations on the Interviewing in the Teacher Apprehension Study," in Paul F. Lazarsfeld and Wagner Thielens, Jr., *The Academic Mind: Social Scientists in a Time of Crisis,* Glencoe, Ill., Free Press, 1958, pp. 266–370. Riesman played virtually all roles in this study: respondent in the sample, analyst of data, and interviewer who followed the interviewers. Mingles observation and analysis of the college professors with reflections on interviewing with characteristic appreciation: "Interviewers in general look younger than their chronological years: only women with a great deal of energy can stand it—and the work keeps them young."

(55) Sidney and Beatrice Webb, *Methods of Social Study,* 1932. Reissued, New York, A. M. Kelley, 1968. Cited appreciatively by both John Madge and Lewis Anthony Dexter for the account of interviewing as an impetus to personal insight and growth.

VI
FOOTNOTES

[1] J. Mayone Stycos, "Interviewer Training in Another Culture," *Public Opinion Quarterly, 16* (2), Summer 1952, 236–246.

[2] Brannon et al. suggest that some of the discrepancy between expressed attitudes and actual behaviors may be the result of the setting in which the attitude is measured when that setting is an artificial one, controlled by an authority figure such as a teacher or researcher. The dictates of random sampling and the odds for eliciting cooperation, which require that the survey *go to* the respondent, may well yield the benefit of greater validity in the content of what is obtained. Research on setting itself seems in order. See R. Brannon et al., "Attitude and Action: A Field Experiment Joined to a General Population Survey," *American Sociological Review,* October, 1973.

[3] An informal measure of students' concern with race was taken in 1967 before they started interviewing. Students were asked to predict how many respondents would report discrimination. Almost all of the students (22 out of 27) anticipated more complaints than blacks actually registered on housing and job discrimination. Students' *mean* guess; that 50 percent of the sample would report discrimination; about 25 percent did.

[4] James L. Norr, Robert B. Zehner, and Stephen J. Cutler, "A Preliminary Examination of Male, Female, and Foreign Student and Professional Interviewer Differences: Detroit Area Study 938." Detroit Area Study, 1969, mimeographed.

[5] This poem and the letters on pages 35–36 were written by Elaine Selo and Carla Shagass in a 1966 paper for the Detroit Area Study.

[6] This is surely Herbert H. Hyman's "intrusive" interviewer. See below.

[7] The specific nature of professional training for interviewers—the inapplicability of nurses' or social workers' training—is discussed by French (13).

[8] If Hyman's work (below) reminds us that we must not exaggerate the consistency in respondents' views, neither must we commit the same error for interviewers. Our feminist concludes her reflections on interviewing, "In general, I found myself embarrassed to be wasting a man's time with questions which were in many cases irrelevant to his frame of reference. I suppose my discomfort arose from a prejudice that men have something important to do all the time, and that everything they do is important. I am convinced that I would have felt more comfortable wasting 90 minutes of a woman's time (if she was a housewife)." Liberationists take note.

9 In his classic work, *Interviewing in Social Research,* Herbert H. Hyman distinguishes between "role expectations" and "attitude-structure expectations" and presents evidence that these two processes are more powerful determinants of interviewer bias than the interviewer's own beliefs or ideology. Hyman's very valuable reexamination of the theory and practice of interviewing proceeds initially from the "phenomenology of the interview"—intensive accounts of their own experience by a small group of experienced interviewers as well as reports of reinterviewing of respondents. See Hyman (15), especially Chapters II and III.

10 David Riesman, in Paul F. Lazarsfeld and Wagner Thielens, Jr., *The Academic Mind,* Glencoe, Ill., Free Press, 1958, p. 305, (54).

11 Asking students their predictions on reports of racial discrimination (described in footnote 3) was such an effort in the Detroit Area Study.

12 We found this process instructive during a recent survey of undergraduates on the issue of cheating. When the students who helped design the questionnaire made their own guesses about the frequency of plagiarizing term papers, they were amazed at how wide-ranging these estimates were: some students thought that the incidence was trivial; others assumed that virtually everyone on campus indulged in the practice. Even in this small group of 30 student-interviewers, the assumptions about other people's behaviors and attitudes were heterogeneous indeed—and the other people in this case were their "own" undergraduate population rather than the cross-section of a metropolitan or national adult population.

13 Stephen A. Richardson, Barbara Dohrenwend, and David Klein, *Interviewing: Its Forms and Functions,* New York, Basic Books, 1965, p. 357, (20).

14 *Ibid.*

15 Angus Campbell, Philip E. Converse, Warren Miller, and Donald E. Stokes, *The American Voter,* New York, Wiley, 1960.

16 Thomas S. Kuhn, *The Structure of Scientific Revolutions,* Chicago, University of Chicago Press, 1962.

17 See Lerner (4).

18 Respondents do not find Detroit Area Study interviewers free with their own opinions. In a follow-up of interviewer performance in 1969, respondents were asked whether interviewers seemed to have opinions themselves, and the answer was overwhelmingly No (95 percent of those responding by mail, which included about half the sample).

19 See Hyman (15) and Schuman and Converse (49).

20 See Dohrenwend (12), Hyman (15), and Weiss (26).

21 Richardson et al., *Interviewing,* pp. 283–284, (20).

22 This material is taken from a paper written for the Detroit Area Study in 1967 by Dawn Day Wachtel.

23 Stanley Milgram, "Some Conditions of Obedience and Disobedience to Authority," *Human Relations, 18* (1), 1965, 67.

24 See Taietz (51) for a systematic analysis of the effects of other persons in the interviewing situation.

25 *Interviewer's Manual,* Ann Arbor, Institute for Social Research, University

of Michigan, 1969, p. 4-1, (25). Our italics. The forthcoming edition of the SRC Manual will reportedly place less stress on rapport building and more on an impersonal, professional approach—consonant with certain aspects of the experimental work of Charles F. Cannell and his associates at the Survey Research Center, and a shift in emphasis that Richardson has found operating more generally in the interviewing field.

[26] Charles H. Backstrom and Gerald Hursh, *Survey Research,* Evanston, Ill., Northwestern University Press, 1963, p. 135.

[27] This material is taken from a paper written for the Detroit Area Study in 1967 by Julianne Oktay, now at Goucher College.

[28] This common-sense assumption needs to be tested. Some relevant experiment is reported in Henson, Cannell, and Lawson (39).

[29] Riesman, in *The Academic Mind,* p. 345, (54).

[30] Few researchers write with the field authority of a David Riesman—or a J. Mayone Stycos, who accompanied some of his interviewers in Jamaica and reported these experiences: "In trying to locate cases, interviewers have been temporarily lost in fields of sugar cane, swept downstream while fording rivers, and drenched in tropical downpours. In one case where I accompanied an interviewer, we climbed rugged, muddy hills for three hours, only to find the respondent not at home." "Proceedings of the American Association for Public Opinion Research," in *Public Opinion Quarterly, 18* (4), Winter 1954–1955, 453.

[31] Coders for the University of Michigan Survey Research Center are required to read the thumbnail sketch before coding any responses.

[32] Donald F. Roy, "The Role of the Researcher in the Study of Social Conflict: A Theory of Protective Distortion of Response," *Human Organization, 24* (3), Fall 1965, 262–271, (21).

[33] Once in a great while, a more charming and discursive letter makes its way to the office, designed to keep the interviewer informed about what's been happening in the family *since* the interview.

[34] W. Donald Rugg relays that over half of the interviewers of the Opinion Research Corporation report that they have at some time been refused an interview because the respondent thought it was a sales pitch. See "Interviewer Opinion on the 'Salesman as Interviewer' Problem," *Public Opinion Quarterly, 35* (4), Winter 1971–1972, 625–626.

[35] Stanley Milgram's concept of "overload" is less fearful but perhaps more general. Urbanites' heightened sense of physical and emotional vulnerability to excessive numbers of contacts with people and problems, as well as to urban crime, leads them to restrict communication with strangers. See "The Experience of Living in Cities," *Science, 167* (3924), March 13, 1970, 1461–1468.

[36] This imagery appeared in an undergraduate's paper relayed to us by Julianne Oktay, who required of her students at Goucher an "interview paper." The experiences reported by her students parallel many of the experiences reported here by Detroit Area Study students, especially the sense of having discovered new dimensions of American experience not available to them in their everyday academic and social life.

37 The refusal rate in 1971 was a bit better, 12.4 percent. Figures for 1972 are not relevant because the sample was based on a set of organizations rather than a metropolitan population. When we gathered data in 1970 for half of those refusing (the other half being unavailable for comment), the front-running explanation given was "all this paper work"—references to the 1970 census long-form, surveys, and bureaucratic paper work of various kinds (27 percent). "Lack of time" was next (14 percent). There was very little evidence for three hypotheses suggested by staff: a "sensitive" racial topic, unusual communication among neighbors, and hostility to students and "campus demonstrations." There were no direct expressions of fearfulness or distrust.

38 In the Milgram article cited above (footnote 35) he reports experimental data on householders' "helpfulness" to strangers asking aid by size of town. Residents of small towns were more willing to admit strangers to use a phone than metropolitan dwellers; the same difference held in a request for helpfulness conducted by telephone in a study reported by Milgram.

39 Interviewers have been known to applaud John Madge's skepticism about the absolute necessity of "learning" this much: "The claim to have collected voluminous, but apparently unusable, material on a variety of deep subjects occurs in research reports so often as to arouse suspicion." Madge, *The Tools of Social Science,* p. 183, footnote, (53). We prefer the explanation that surveys are often long, or even overlong, because investigators are aware that part of what they ask will not pan out but they do not know in advance which part.

40 But the process may also reflect what Freedman and Fraser call the "foot-in-the-door" effect. Respondents willing to devote a modest amount of time may be more likely, later, to agree to a more substantial amount. The same thing probably goes with respect to questions: it seems to be easier to ask sensitive questions later in the interview after some commitment to the interviewer or the process has been generated. See Jonathan L. Freedman and Scott C. Fraser, "Compliance Without Pressure: The Foot-in-the-Door Technique," in Leonard Bickman and Thomas Henchy, *Beyond the Laboratory: Field Research in Social Psychology,* New York, McGraw-Hill Book Company, 1972, pp. 71–77.

41 For a classic statement of this criticism, see Herbert Blumer, "The Mass, the Public, and Public Opinion," in *Reader in Public Opinion and Communication,* edited by Bernard Berelson and Morris Janowitz, 2nd ed., New York, Free Press, 1966, pp. 43–50.

42 See Riesman and Benney, "The Sociology of the Interview" (47).

43 See Shapiro (22) for an analysis of variation in open-ended answers.

44 Leo Bogart, "No Opinion, Don't Know, and Maybe No Answer," *Public Opinion Quarterly, 31* (3), Fall 1967, 337, (30).

45 See Sicinski (23).

46 See Converse (33).

47 The basic interpretation in both Henson et al. (39) and Marquis et al. (41) focuses on a tendency of better-educated persons to lose some of the challenge to adequate task performance under conditions of greater interviewer reinforce-

ment or personalism. The quoted material of Henson et al. is from the "Discussion," pp. 51–55.

[48] Riesman, in *The Academic Mind*, p. 352, footnote, (54).

[49] See Miller (18).

[50] There is also evidence that too much "distance" generates its form of interviewer effect. Dohrenwend et al. set forth a conceptualization of the problem that seems especially interesting and useful. See (12).

[51] Richardson et al., *Interviewing*, p. 283, (20).

[52] Researchers may deem our faith unwarranted that such practices are really possible, and it does reflect a high degree of acceptance of interviewers' own evaluation of their performance in this instance at least. We must admit, with Richardson, that "The foregoing discussion assumes that the interviewer can vary at will the type of interpersonal role he plays in order to adopt the role congenial to the respondent. Unfortunately, there has been little examination of this question in the interview literature. The evidence cited . . . suggests that there is considerable variation in the flexibility of interviewers . . . and limitations on the degree to which interviewers can adapt their behavior to that of different respondents." *Op. cit.,* p. 327. Only *virtuosi* need apply.

[53] Anxious beginners often consider the merits of paying respondents for their time. For reasons of frugality, we have never instituted such an experiment, but there is some evidence that money is neither necessary nor particularly helpful. See Dohrenwend (11).

[54] The interviewer would nevertheless be gratified by Philip E. Converse's reflections on his own experience as a respondent. When asked questions to which he brings little prior thought or interest, Converse finds himself feeling something on the order of "test fatigue" as a "direct consequence of pressures . . . to search for faint or non-existent bits of affect" with which to fulfill the demand for an attitude. "In those rare cases when an attitude item or battery dovetails nicely with thoughts or feelings I have experienced on my own with any strength or clarity before, even such an impersonal process as marking a questionnaire offers the reward of pleasant catharsis. Such pleasure seems somewhat infrequent, however, and the hunt-and-fabricate feeling is fully as familiar. One outcome of such harassment is fatigue; another is a more or less conscious recourse to some response set touched off more by question form than question content." If human beings generally have a huge and "vibrant bundle of attitudes" on all manner of subjects, Converse finds that he himself does not, and in complying with the demands of survey research generates his share of "nonattitudes." One strategy he suggests for the general problem is ascertaining the level of information the respondent brings to a given topic. See Converse, "Attitudes and Non-Attitudes: Continuation of a Dialogue," (33) especially p. 177.

[55] Interviewers are not above joining the chorus of criticism from outsiders, so familiar to researchers in the field: measuring attitudes does not predict behaviors; interviewing individuals does not capture the complex interaction of people in groups or organizations; asking people questions does not deal with the

contingencies and imponderables of real life; adding up attitudes does not render the "whole man"; surveying opinions may actually create opinions. Herbert McClosky confesses to weariness with these shopworn charges but patiently answers them nevertheless. See (42).

[56] Quoted by John Madge, *The Tools of Social Science,* p. 238, from Sidney and Beatrice Webb, *Methods of Social Study,* London, 1932, p. 137. But lest we affect too much humility, let us counter the interviewers' judgment about the choice of pretest respondents. The most useful pretest sample is surely a cross section or a truly random one—a choice usually precluded by cost. Interviewers much prefer the opposite extreme, trying out questions on their (much-interviewed?) family and friends, a nonrepresentative group indeed. This is not mere sloth, of course: calling on prospective respondents without an advance letter is usually a wearying, refusal-ridden business. Detroit Area Study interviewers are nevertheless required to pretest by calling on strangers, door to door, "sampled" only in that the areas of a city has been specified in advance. This assignment is usually tougher than the final interviewing itself but that extra hazard would seem to offer useful, realistic interviewing experience as well as a good hurdle for questions.

[57] Richardson et al., *Interviewing,* p. 149, (20). Richardson's view of the low-status subordinate is at some variance with the view of the Webbs, just cited. Edith Fein (38) contends from another perspective that it is the survey researcher who fails to grasp the *respondent's* purpose in coping with his own lower-class life. All three implied definitions of lower status are just general enough that there is probably no real disagreement among the three authors cited.

[58] The woman's very individual approach to religious identification is a statistical rarity, but one can share the interviewer's admiration for her views: "No, I don't really have a religious preference. I am a formal member of the Catholic church—for my husband. But I think the Church as an institution is not as God would want people to worship Him. He has no preference, so why should I? I worship in many churches. I once went to a Baptist convention of liturgy. When I was asked at the altar if I wanted to join the church—two women had taken my hand to lead me forward—I said that I would in *spirit.* Being a member does not necessarily establish a preference. Put down *None.*"

[59] See Schuman (48).

[60] Inkeles reports a survey procedure in which interviewers indicated (by check marks) the number of times it was necessary to repeat a given question to a respondent. See Alex Inkeles and David H. Smith, *Becoming Modern* (forthcoming).

[61] See Back and Gergen (28). In general, the closed alternatives may be used in a question precisely in order to confront the respondent with something that he might not otherwise volunteer.

[62] Elisabeth Noelle-Neumann, "Wanted: Rules for Wording Structured Questionnaires," *Public Opinion Quarterly, 34* (2), Summer 1970, 194, (43).

[63] Examples are given in Payne (44) and Noelle-Neumann (43). Some effects from question *order* are analyzed by Daniel H. Willick and Richard K. Ashley,

"Survey Question Order and Political Party Preferences of College Students and Their Parents," *Public Opinion Quarterly, 35* (2), Summer 1971, 189–199.

[64] This material is taken from a paper written for the Detroit Area Study, "The Rational Approach to Racism," by Karen Schwab in 1968. She is now at Rutgers University.

[65] Riesman, *The Academic Mind,* p. 291, (54).

[66] See Marquis et al. (41). Considerable extra training was required to equip interviewers with a set of "reinforcement" comments that could be used for experimental variation and that were at once natural, appropriate, and standardized for a variety of situations.

[67] Pool, "A Critique of the Twentieth Anniversary Issue," p. 193 (45).

[68] Bogart, p. 344 (30).

[69] Madge, *The Tools of Social Science,* p. 248 (53).

[70] Cannell and Kahn, "Interviewing," p. 586 (9). The reference to John Dewey is *Democracy in Education,* New York, Macmillan, 1916.

[71] Cannell and Kahn, *op. cit.,* p. 587 (9).

VII
APPENDIX: ON MATTERS OF TRAINING

Ideas that interviewers have offered about the interviewer-training aspects of survey research are sprinkled throughout the text. We collect them here, referenced by page number, adding some brief comments on other training practices that have seemed useful and that have evoked some enthusiasm from interviewers as well.

None of the above beats actual practice. We share Cannell and Kahn's sense that in "every type of skill training people rediscover the old dictum of John Dewey that training is not so much a matter of telling someone how to do something as of providing him with opportunities to do it —to participate actively in practicing the skill he wishes to attain." [70]

As a rule, however, only the largest survey organizations, blessed with permanent field staff, are able to put that old dictum to maximum use. Most academic surveys have to lean at least somewhat, and often heavily, on verbal instruction, group discussion, and examples of good and bad practice from transcribed or taped interviews, mixed with as many opportunities for practice as the limited budget and personnel will allow. The ideas collected here are addressed to individuals who must depend at least as much on the discussion and simulated practice of the training class as on the actual experience of the much more instructive field.

1. Researchers should interview

The "bias" of interviewers on this score is blatant enough in the text —and we share it. Researchers can get much illumination from trying out their pretest themselves. When they fail to allow time for it, they sacrifice another potential asset as well: their interviewers' sense that these researchers are hardy spirits, with some down-to-earth appreciation of field conditions—precisely what our regrettable assistant on page 33 seemed to lack (a deficiency that the interviewer headed home for her martini on page 64 apparently suspected of *most* researchers).

2. Enhancing the initial confidence of interviewers

(a) *Advance letter*

This is such a common practice now that it probably bears only a mention. Interviewers heartily approve of the procedure. The effect on their initial confidence (not to mention their final response rate) seems benign indeed.

(b) *Notification of police or other governmental officials*

This, too, is common and, as good luck usually has it, rarely needed. Knowing that somebody in City Hall can certify to the interviewer's legitimacy, if the need should arise, is nevertheless a help.

(c) *Discussion of the incomplete explanation*

The advance letter, or the doorstep explanation, rarely tells the whole story. Some interviewers (especially students) feel that the initial information to the respondent is so vague or incomplete as to constitute a virtual deception, which makes them uneasy or skeptical. Tracing out in discussion some of the problems of giving a complete explanation of the survey has helped interviewers to think through the prospects for biasing the views of respondents or biasing the sample itself. For example, explaining to respondents that we wish to investigate plagiarism among college students may well decrease the supply of the very people of most interest to us, the plagiarizers and their supporters who approve. Similarly, explaining forthrightly that our main research interest is in racial attitudes is likely to change in some (unknown) way the numbers and kinds of people we are able to interview, or the *set* they bring to the questions. Restless interviewers of good conscience need to make some distinction between outright deception and incomplete explanation that is used to avoid bias, lest they proceed into actual interviewing feeling somehow compromised and faintly dishonest.

(d) *Offering a report of results*

Many survey organizations now make it a practice to reciprocate a respondent's time and thought by sending out a short summary of results to persons who wish it. Although there is usually a fair time-lag between the interviewing and the report—the few who have forgotten the interview must be puzzled when they get the results—it pleases interviewers to offer it, especially beginners who feel that they are intruding or imposing on respondents. We cannot vouch for readership, but many people do take us up on the offer.

(e) What respondents get out of it

The summary on pages 52–59 can be enriched by discussion with experienced professional interviewers, if that is possible. Otherwise, beginners can bring their own impressions of the pretest experience back for discussion.

3. Adequate and complete asking of the questions

(a) Mere reading aloud

As simpleminded as this suggestion seems, it is not always featured in the early training period and it seems to be useful in making interviewers sensitive to errors in actual reading, as well as in emphasis, tone, and naturalness.

(b) Checking out the "unaskable"

Some interviewers come to training with various bits of conventional wisdom about what one *cannot* say; for example, to cite some very true confessions, one cannot ask a man his income, a woman her age, or a black how he feels about whites (if one is white). Such convictions should be allowed to surface in discussion so that the researcher can deal with them—citing research findings, where available, on the actual response rate for such "sensitive" questions. If interviewers keep these views entirely private, they may just privately resolve to skip the "impossible" questions and supply their own best guess.

4. Avoiding the stereotyping of respondents

We cannot improve upon the suggestions summarized on pages 16–18, except to guess that these exercises are most profitable between pretesting and final interviewing, when one has gathered a few impressions of respondents with which to start constructing grand generalizations.

5. Introduction on the doorstep

If the interviewer is armed with the prospect of an advance letter, police notification, hard rules about appropriate interviewing hours, and thorough knowledge of the questionnaire, he can probably do no better than to have a "sample introduction"—and practice in trying it out, even in class. No written introduction prepared by staff—no "canned heartiness" in Cannell and Kahn's felicitous phrase—will really substitute for a straightforward introduction in the interviewer's own style.

But this will come, as he works. For beginners, the first step in practice is just getting *something* out, a canned speech or anything that is mildly relevant. Class practice is a place to start.

6. Refusals and interviews

To the counsel of interviewers on pages 36–45, we would add only two other specific items: (a) the usefulness of role-playing the refuser or reluctant respondent, as well as the interviewer; (b) the occasional utility of making it clear to a resister at the outset that he can refuse to answer any questions that he finds objectionable. The offer must be genuine, although ordinarily if a respondent consents to the interview at all, he is likely to balk at few of the questions. This is another instance of reducing pressure by focusing on the respondent's choice, discussed in another context on page 29.

In the training class, current rates of refusals for the organization or the topic should be discussed candidly. See pages 40–41. If possible, an experienced professional interviewer should be invited to such a discussion, not only for specific suggestions but also for the manifest long-term success that he or she represents.

Suggestions for getting the interview, pages 41–45, can be supplemented by discussion of pretest experiences.

7. Verbatim transcription

Training manuals invariably counsel interviewers to make verbatim transcriptions of the respondent's answers—without shortening, without paraphrasing. The point usually merits strong emphasis and actual practice in the training class. The distinction between a verbatim record and a paraphrase would seem to be obvious enough, but it has been our experience that without training practice, a few interviewers will fail to apply the distinction and return questionnaires that read this way: "He said that he violently disagreed with the government's policy to cut social security payments," or some such transmission of the interviewer's mind and language, not the respondent's. Reading off long answers at a realistically conversational pace, asking interviewers to transcribe them, and then comparing the transcriptions has proved a useful class exercise. It certainly makes the recording problem vivid and has tended to sensitize interviewers to the paraphrase errors.

In cautioning interviewers against taking editorial liberties, three reasons seem worth stressing:

(a) The coder needs the real thing—a record of the respondent's language and thought, not the interviewer's. What the respondent actually said (duly probed for intention, meaning, specificity) is the
best possible guide to his thought or feeling. If the interviewer
judges that additional interpretation would be helpful to the coder,
a note of explanation should be added in parenthesis; interpretation should not intervene *between* the respondent and the coder.

(b) Contextual or linguistic analysis of open-ended material will prove
impossible if answers have been paraphrased or condensed. Interviewers cannot anticipate the full range of information that researchers may ultimately seek from the data. At some later date,
researchers may wish to examine answers for specific casts of mind
or turns of phrase—racial terms, political phrases, references to
group identities, or the like. If interviewers have varied in their
conscientiousness about recording the literal language, such analysis is hopelessly compromised.

(c) Survey research is now old and rich enough in data to merit in-
valuable historical and regional analysis of open-ended material.
An interviewer's bland paraphrase will blur the rich differences in
a sharecropper of the 1930s, a Korean war veteran of the 1950s,
an electronics engineer or a women's liberationist of the 1970s,
and how they felt about their life and time.

All these reasons apply most fully and powerfully to the open questions devised by the researcher precisely to capture the respondent's
own turn of thought. Here it is crucial for the interviewer to record in
true and literal detail the respondent's every word. At the other extreme, we feel that it is legitimate to pare down comments that are ex-
traneous or supplementary to an alternative already clearly chosen in
response to a closed question. The most conscientious (and speedy) interviewers sometimes mass all questionnaire margins with verbatim
transcriptions of *everything* the respondent says. The material is rarely
without interest for any reader of questionnaires; but because it is com-
pletely unstandardized, it can hardly ever be used in conventional data
analysis. Here, we think, interviewers can be allowed to transcribe the
essential ideas and expressions (in the respondent's own words, as
ever), letting the superfluous and repetitious go. Doing so is no mean
skill. In between these two clear-cut and frequent cases are occasional
responses to closed questions that do not obviously fit the stated alternatives of the questionnaire. Exact and full transcription is highly desirable here to allow for later coding or recoding decisions, but with a
very voluble respondent, hell-bent to avoid categories, some paring may
be inevitable.

Class exercises in practice transcription should be keyed to training the interviewer in distinguishing between the actual answer, which must be transcribed in full, and the marginal comment, which can be shortened to critical words and phrases.

8. Practice-interviewing

(a) *The utility of strangers*

If the survey organization does not administer pretests door-to-door, as described on page 98, the individual interviewer should be charged with finding a stranger on his own. Interviewing family or friends is useful, and may be a prior step, but it should not serve as sufficient practice-experience, either for the pretesting of the questionnaire or the tempering of the interviewer's skill.

(b) *Taped interviews*

Recording of actual interviews can usually be elicited from among the most confident of the trainees who are not likely to be daunted by candid discussion of strengths and weaknesses of the interviews. They may be relatively inhibited performances—in which the interviewer is perhaps more cool and impersonal than he or she will be in the real, unrecorded setting—but the value of any performance is incontestable. Cannell and Kahn's caution about a supportive training environment is particularly germane here: "[The interviewer] must know that his clumsiest efforts will not excite ridicule, that the worst of his early mistakes will bring help rather than blame, that the others in the situation share and understand his problems." [71]

9. Probing for more complete information

(a) *With neutrality*

Even after interviewers are duly instructed in a full "probing script," a short version of which is mentioned on pages 50–51, class practice usually reveals that the unbiased probe is fairly tricky for interviewers at the beginning. Role playing has been helpful here, even in the oversimplified form of presenting a few moments of questionnaire dialogue, and then at a problematic point, asking each interviewer to intervene with a nondirective probe of his own invention. Discussion of what distinguishes a neutral probe from a biased one is essential, and examples should be abundant. (The simple exercise described above usually turns up abundant examples of bias.)

(b) For specificity

1. Code construction. A useful brief training exercise in probing incorporates something of Lester Guest's procedure of providing interviews with practice coding (14). We have distributed, to interviewers, all the answers to a given pretest question and asked them to participate in constructing a set of categories that could be used to code all the collected answers. (This is not the actual code we will ultimately use—the code rarely being in respectable shape at the time of initial interview training.) Inevitably interviewers find that some of the answers that seemed entirely reasonable on the scene just cannot be coded: they are virtually without content and must be dumped into the unenlightening departments of "other" or "not ascertained." By self-report, and by impressionistic evidence in subsequent pretests, this has helped interviewers to sharpen their sense of the hopelessly general answer, especially ones for which they unconsciously provided their *own* meaning and content on the spot.

2. Coding of pretest responses. Coding of a pretest serves a similar function. It seems most instructive to have each interviewer code others' questionnaires and report to discussion the problems he encountered.

(c) For "Don't Know"

As mentioned on page 50 and page 69, it is useful for more standardized interviewing procedures if researchers set down some guidelines about how many times the interviewer should press ignorance or uncertainty. The variable meaning of Don't Know (pages 49–50) merits fair emphasis in training.

(d) Field supervision in probing

The suggestion that interviewers evaluate each other's open-ended answers in pairs (page 49) seems a useful supplement to supervisors' doing so, certainly for the first two or three genuine interviews, if possible.

10. Cutting the conversation

See pages 45–48. Again, role playing seems most useful for gaining practice of this kind.

11. Mild discomfort versus serious distress

As discussed on pages 28–30, interviewers and researchers together must share a common culture about what constitutes serious invasion of a respondent's privacy or composure since this will vary to a certain extent with the nature of the inquiry. For the rare interview that must be broken off by these criteria, it is useful for interviewers to have some sense of question priority; for example, we have sometimes found it important to urge interviewers to make every effort to get the basic demographic data, even if some crisis arises that makes the skipping of some portion of the questionnaire a regrettable necessity.

12. Morale in the field

(a) Interviewing the interviewers

The pleasures of being a respondent (see page 55 ff.) should be accorded to off-duty interviewers, too, when they require a sympathetic audience now and then from among their own ranks or from the research staff. Researchers who show little curiosity about respondents, harrowing working conditions, or meritorious efforts in the call of duty are truly exasperating and downright disheartening to some interviewers. Researchers often need to *instruct* their assistants in the virtues of listening—with interest. See pages 32–35.

(b) Group contact

The collected suggestions on this matter appear on pages 35–36. *Inexpensive* variants on the notions can probably be devised for some studies.

13. The thumbnail sketch

Not every survey requires such a description of the respondent, by any means, but it has many uses (even for validating the interview, on occasion). Since interviewers usually vary in their measure of literary ability that can "sketch" a situation or a personality in a few words, they should be instructed in the aspects of greatest interest to the researcher. The least literary will get *those,* while the most literary will get much more. The most artful sketches can be recycled back into training procedures designed to dilute the researcher's bias (page 32 ff.) and the interviewer's expectations (pages 17–18).

14. Forestalling fake interviews

We have saved this "tasteless" subject for last, not because we are totally inexperienced in such sorrows but because "survey research as interviewers see it" barely gives it a mention.

Our own practice generally proceeds on one theory of prevention.

We often get phone numbers from respondents so that a small sample of interviews can be verified by a supervisor. (The interviewer is to explain this directly.) On very rare occasions we have even made house calls. Most important, as we see it, is explaining this plan to interviewers at the outset; it is clear that some fraction of the interviewers' work will be checked.

Another process amounts to something like scratching the *finish* of an interviewer to see if a believable person shows beneath. Gossip in the trade has it that one very inventive cheat (ultimately apprehended, we are pleased to report) was a doctoral candidate in psychology *and* a practicing novelist. Most of us do not have all the professional credentials and talents to "make up" people with all the variety, uniqueness, inconsistency, and complexity of the real thing—which brings us full circle to the theme with which we opened this book.

AUTHOR INDEX

Numbers in parentheses indicate reference numbers or footnotes.

Ashley, Richard K., 98(63)

Back, Hurt W., 69, 83(6,7), 87(28), 88(37), 98(61)
Backstrom, Charles H., 83(8), 95(26)
Becker, Howard S., 87(29)
Benney, Mark, 91(47), 96(42)
Blumer, Herbert, 96(41)
Bogart, Leo, 50, 74−75, 87(30), 96(44), 99(68)
Brannon, R., 93(2)

Campbell, Angus, 94(15)
Cannell, Charles F., 53, 54, 84(9), 85(17), 87(31,32), 89(39,41), 95(25,28), 96(47), 99(66,70,71), 100, 102, 105
Colombotos, John, 84(12), 97(50)
Converse, Jean M., 24, 91(49), 94(19)
Converse, Philip E., 20, 50, 88(33), 94(15), 96(46), 97(54)
Cutler, Stephen J., 93(4)

Dewey, John, 99(70), 100
Dexter, Lewis Anthony, 82(1), 84(10), 88 (34)
Dohrenwend, Barbara Snell, 84(11, 12), 86(20), 88(35, 36), 94(13, 20, 21), 97(50, 51,53), 98(57)
Dohrenwend, Bruce, 84(12), 97(50)

Ehrlich, June Sachar, 91(52)

Fallaci, Oriana, 83(3)
Fein, Edith, 89(38), 98(57)
Fraser, Scott C., 96(40)
Freedman, Jonathan L., 96(40)
French, Kathrine S., 84(13), 93(7)

Gergen, Kenneth J., 69, 87(28), 88(37), 98 (61)
Glazer, Nathan, 90(46)
Gorden, Raymond L., 82(2)
Guest, Lester, 85(14)

Henson, Ramon, 53, 54, 89(39), 95(28), 96(47)
Hill, Reuben, 83(6)
Hursh, Gerald D., 83(8), 95(26)
Hyman, Herbert H., 24, 85(15), 93(6,8), 94(9,19,20)

Inkeles, Alex, 98(60)

Junker, Buford H., 85(16)

Kahn, Robert L., 84(9), 85(17), 99(70,71), 100, 102, 105
Klein, David, 86(20), 94(13,21), 97(51), 98(57)
Kuhn, Thomas S., 20, 94(16)

Laurent, Andre, 87(31), 89(41), 96(47), 99(66)
Lawson, Sally (Robison), 53, 54, 89(39), 95(28), 96(47). *See also* Robison, Sally
Lazarsfeld, Paul F., 89(40)
Lerner, Daniel, 22, 83(4), 94(17)

McClosky, Herbert, 89(42), 98(55)
Madge, John, 79−80, 92(53), 96(39), 98 (56), 99(69)
Marquis, Kent H., 87(31), 89(41), 96(47), 99(66)
Milgram, Stanley, 28, 94(23), 95(35), 96(38)
Miller, S. M., 54, 85(18), 97(49)

109

SUBJECT INDEX

Numbers in parentheses indicate reference numbers or footnotes.

Conduct of interview, administrative preparations for, 101
  digressions, 45–48, 61–62
  faked, 107–108
  introduction, 36, 102–103
  pacing to respondent's needs, 29
  probing, 48–54, 62, 86(22), 105–106
  quality of, estimated, 5
  rapport, 54, 86(26)
  report of results, 101
  setting, 2–5, 91(51), 93(2)
  sketch of respondent, 34, 95(31), 107
  time-length, 42, 96(39)
  training, see Interviewer role
  transcription, 103–105

Interviewer bias, through expectations, 16–18, 85(15), 93(3), 94(11,12)
  through interpersonal effects, 85(15,18), 86(26), 87(28), 90(45)
  through interviewer characteristics, 23–24, 84(12), 85(15), 91(49,51,52), 97(50)
  through interviewer opinions, 12–13
  through stereotyping, 13–16, 85(15)
Interviewer role, anxiety of beginners, 11–12, 42–44
  conflicts in, 25–26, 30–32, 60
  ethical considerations, 27–30, 42, 84(10), 85(19), 101, 106–107
  flexibility, see Interviewer style
  learning stages, 10–22, 59–60
  morale, 33–36, 83(7), 100, 107
  neutrality, 7–8, 12–20, 23–24, 62, 87

(29), 88(34), 88(36), 94(18), 102
  personal growth through, 8–9, 19–21, 79–81, 92(53,54,55)
  satisfaction, 7, 18–21
  training, 83(6,7), 85(14), 98(56), 100–108
Interviewer style, variation in, 27, 50–55, 62, 89(39,41), 92(52), 97(52)

Questions, adequacy of, 27, 65–69, 97(54)
  effects from form of, 53, 69, 89(39), 90(43,44), 98(63)
  open and closed, 66–69, 77, 88(35), 89(40), 91(49)
  pretesting, 65–66, 98(56)
  sensitive, 102
  variety, 70–72, 90(43)

Refusals, methods of overcoming, 36–45, 61, 96(40), 103
  rates of, 40, 96(37)
  reasons for, 36–40, 95(34,35), 96(38)
Respondents, differential understanding, 89(38), 91(47,50)
  motivation, 22–25, 55–59, 62–63, 65, 70–71, 84(11), 97(53), 102
  nonopinion, 49–50, 62, 86(23), 87(30), 88(33,37), 97(54)

Survey researchers, criticisms of, 44, 64–65, 70–75, 89(38,42), 97(55)
  field experience, 86(24), 95(30), 100
  technical bias, 33–35
  rational bias, 72–75, 77